# *My Christian Journey with Zen*

Gustav Ericsson

Calligraphy Paintings by Gudo Nishijima Roshi

Calligraphy paintings by Gudo Nishijima Roshi, Tokyo, 2007. Used with permission.
Front cover photo of the Maria Kannon statue in the rock garden at Shinmeizan, Japan. Photo by the author.
Back cover photo by Magnus Ericsson.

All Shobogenzo quotations are taken from *Master Dogen's Shobogenzo*, volumes 1–4, translated by Gudo Nishijima and Chodo Cross (Tokyo: Windbell Publications, 1994, 1996, 1997, and 1999), and *Master Dogen's Shinji Shobogenzo*, translated by Gudo Nishijima and edited by Michael Luetchford and Jeremy Pearson (Tokyo: Windbell Publications, 2003).

All Bible quotations are taken from the Holy Bible, New International Version (NIV). Copyright © 1973, 1978, 1984, 2011 by Biblica, Inc. Used by permission of Zondervan. All rights reserved worldwide (www.zondervan.com). The New International Version or NIV are trademarks registered in the US Patent and Trademark Office by Biblica, Inc.

*My Christian Journey with Zen* was first published in 2015. This slightly revised edition was published in 2020.

For further information and to get in touch with the author, visit: www.anzenkai.com.

For Alfred, August and Edvard

# Table of Contents

Preface .................................................... vii
Chapter One         A Traveler in Search of a Sword ........ 1
Chapter Two         One Look at the Peach Blossoms ....... 9
Chapter Three       Naked Mind at the
                    Present Moment ...................... 15
Chapter Four        Only the Act of Sitting................. 31
Chapter Five        The Sky Doesn't
                    Hinder the Clouds..................... 63
Chapter Six         A Child of Fire
                    Comes to Get Fire .................... 73
Chapter Seven       Not to Know Is the Most
                    Direct and Familiar ................... 81
Chapter Eight       The Moaning of Dragons among
                    Withered Trees ....................... 91
Chapter Nine        There Is No One
                    Who Doesn't Hear Them.............. 97
Chapter Ten         All those Who Hear It Free
                    Themselves of Something ............ 107
Chapter Eleven      The Whole Universe Is
                    One Brilliant Pearl.................... 115
Chapter Twelve      Anzenkai ............................. 121
Acknowledgments ......................................... 127
Calligraphy References ................................... 129

# Preface

Outside the window, everything is white. There is snow everywhere, and we have shoveled the path to our front door several times in the last couple of days. I don't know if the historical Jesus or Buddha ever experienced how silent it is after a heavy snowfall, or if they had a chance to see kids jump in the snowdrifts. I guess not, but thousands of years later, far up in the snow land of northern Sweden, I don't know who I would have been without their lives and legacies.

The meeting of Christianity and Buddhism has been a heart matter to me throughout my adult life. Since I graduated from high school in 1997, I have been on a journey to explore this meeting and dialogue, which has led me to travels and retreats, especially in Japan. In the spring of 2012, I returned to Japan to write about my experiences. I visited temples, churches, and friends, and some of my daily travel notes became the basic structure of this book. The next year, I went back again with my family for more input and writing, and I continued to work on the chapters now and then for a couple of years back home.

What I have ended up with is not a comprehensive story but a patchwork of reflections and glimpses into my Christian journey with Zen. When I take a step back and look at what I have written, I believe the main theme is how I learned meditation and what it has become in my life and in my work as a hospital priest in the Evangelical Lutheran Church of Sweden.

My Japanese Zen teacher, Gudo Nishijima Roshi, died on January 28, 2014, and this book is a way for me to remember him, what he taught, and the time we had together. Nishijima was a devoted reader and translator of Dogen Zenji's collected works, the Shobogenzo, as well as Dogen's Shinji Shobogenzo, which is a collection of short stories, usually conversations, called cases, or *koan* in Japanese.

Dogen was a Japanese Buddhist monk in the thirteenth century who traveled to study and practice Zen, called Chan in Chinese, with teachers in China and then returned and established the Soto Zen tradition in Japan, in which I have had most of my meditation training.

Nishijima painted several quotes from the Shobogenzo and Shinji Shobogenzo in calligraphy for me. On my trips to Japan in 2012 and 2013, I brought images of his calligraphic works with me. I reflected on them along the way, and they have now become titles for the chapters in this book.

Each chapter begins with one of Nishijima's calligraphy paintings and ends with a short passage from the Bible. Please note that I'm using metaphors, expressions, and stories from different traditions, without any claim to the correct version or understanding. My intention with this book isn't about right or wrong, and I have tried to keep it as short as possible—with enough structure for it to be readable and with enough mess left for it to be honest. I want to share what has been helpful to me along the way, and I hope you will enjoy it.

Gustav Ericsson
Umeå, February 10, 2015

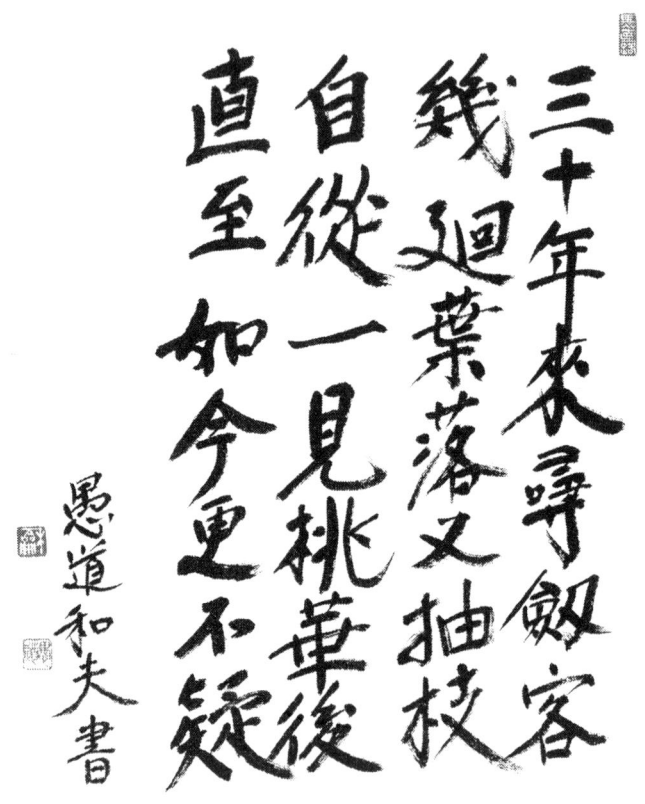

*For thirty years, a traveler in search of a sword.*
*How many times have leaves fallen and buds sprouted?*

# Chapter One
# A Traveler in Search of a Sword

*Sunday, April 22, 2012*
I landed at Narita Airport this morning, and I'm writing from a small hotel room on the eighteenth floor in Tokyo. Through the window, I see millions of city lights and a horizon of buildings. It's been eleven years since I came here for the first time, as a theology student searching for a Zen teacher. Leaves have fallen and buds have sprouted many times since then. Now the streets below me are calming down in the Tokyo night. Now and then there is the sound of sirens.

―

I was born in 1978 in Umeå, in the northern part of Sweden, and I grew up in a safe and loving family with my mother, father, and two younger brothers. When I was about five years old, my parents took me to a nearby children's church group. At the church, I heard about a man in a land far away, a long time ago. He was born in a simple stable in Bethlehem, under a bright, shining star, and he grew up with his parents in a town called Nazareth in Galilee. I heard that he was the Son of God, and I saw images and listened to stories of how he helped those who were sick and oppressed. But some people did not like what he did, and he was imprisoned and condemned to death. He suffered and died, nailed to a cross, but he rose from the grave. I was a little child, but some of the stories and images stayed with me. Little did I know that I would travel far east before returning to him again.

In accordance with the tradition of the Church of Sweden, I was baptized when I was a few months old and then confirmed when I was about fourteen years old. Before confirmation, I had to learn by heart the prayer that Jesus of Nazareth taught his disciples two thousand years ago as part of the Sermon on the Mount (Matt. 6:9–13). I remember that I used to say it repeatedly sometimes when I rode my bike home, as fast as I could, through dark and forested areas that scared me at night:

> Our Father, who art heaven,
> hallowed be thy name;
> thy kingdom come;
> thy will be done;

on earth as it is in heaven.
Give us this day our daily bread.
And forgive us our trespasses,
as we forgive those who trespass against us.
And lead us not into temptation;
but deliver us from evil.
For thine is the kingdom,
the power, and the glory
for ever and ever.
Amen.

But I couldn't really connect with the church and its teachings. They seemed strange and irrational to me and left me feeling frustrated. Then I learned more about the painful parts of my family's history. Several of my relatives suffered from disease. My dear grandmothers died, and I saw my parents grieve. I became angry with the God I had heard about in church, and I remember thinking seriously to myself that if I ever got the chance, I would do my best to punch God for all the suffering.

About a year after confirmation, gnawing existential questions led me to the bookshelves at the library and at home. For some reason, I couldn't let go of religion. I found books on Hinduism and Buddhism, as well as poetry collections, and I read with great interest. One of my favorite poems from the Zen Buddhist tradition begins with these lines:

> For thirty years, a traveler in search of a sword.
> How many times have leaves fallen and buds sprouted?

When I was about sixteen years old, I began feeling something like a traveler in search of a sword. I was living a safe and comfortable life, but like many of my peers, I was struggling with identity, relationships, and existential questions, trying to find my way and place in the world. I wanted to find something that could help me cut through the inner difficulties I was experiencing. I felt as if something important was lacking, and that I needed to solve the puzzle.

A small Krishna temple and vegetarian restaurant called Govinda's opened in Umeå. For about three years, I went there almost every Sunday afternoon to listen to the resident devotee, Yogindra Prabhu. He would lecture to the group on a verse from the Hindu sacred text the Bhagavad Gita, and then we would sing old devotional mantras in Sanskrit with him. He quoted from the Gita and said that everything rests upon God, like pearls are strung on a thread (Bhagavad Gita 7:7).

Yogindra taught bhakti yoga as a path to transcend the miseries of this world by training one's heart and mind in loving devotion (Bhagavad Gita 18:65), first and foremost by chanting and singing the ancient mantra:

Hare Krishna
Hare Krishna
Krishna Krishna
Hare Hare
Hare Rama
Hare Rama
Rama Rama
Hare Hare

I got the chaplets with 108 wooden beads and would practice mantra meditation from time to time. The Hare Krishna movement gave me something practical and different from the Christian world I had found frustrating, and it made me feel connected with something that was compelling to me.

From my high school, it was only a five-minute walk to Govinda's. At almost every school lunch break, my friend Martin and I would walk to the temple to eat vegetarian Indian food that had first been offered to Krishna, called *prasadam*. Yogindra and our parents made an arrangement: for a small amount of money every semester, Martin and I could have lunch every day at the temple instead of our high school dining hall. Sometimes I also brought home food from Govinda's to our family dinners.

I didn't formally join the Hare Krishna movement, but Yogindra talked about God in a way that I could connect to. Much of what I experienced at the temple inspired me. For example, I heard a story about a thirsty camel in the desert. The camel found a cactus and, in desperation, began chewing on one of its thorns. The thorn caused the camel's mouth to bleed, but the blood felt like water, so he swallowed it and continued to chew on the thorn. It was a disturbing image, and the story stayed with me. I wanted to find real water and not live my life like that camel.

Frustration and feelings of existential alienation kept gnawing at me, and then a long-term relationship came to a painful end. I felt depressed and began dreaming of escaping to a different life as a Buddhist monk, far away in the Himalaya Mountains.

My friend Fredrik and I saved our money, and when we were nineteen years old, after we had graduated from high school, we bought plane tickets to Nepal. We went to Kopan, a Tibetan Buddhist monastery in the Kathmandu Valley. At Kopan, I asked one of the monks in the red and-yellow robes about meditation, and he suggested that I sit down and explore the question "Who am I?" I wanted to know more, but he smiled and said that just exploring this question would last a lifetime.

Nepal was colorful and beautiful to me in many ways, but the foreign culture and religious practices made me feel more lost than ever. The poverty overwhelmed me, and some images remain burned in my memory: little girls with dirty clothes and small babies in their arms, pulling my clothes and begging for money, with tears running from their eyes. A sick man bleeding from his mouth, begging for our coins. Fredrik and I gave some of what we had to them. We didn't talk much about what we had witnessed. Neither of us had ever seen anything like that before, and we were both shaken by the suffering that we saw at some places in Kathmandu.

Nepal was different from my idealistic fantasies. What I had tried to escape from in Sweden had followed me there. Late one night in the monastery, I lay awake. For the first time, I thought about returning to the Church of Sweden and giving it another try. That night, I even fantasized about becoming a priest.

After just a few weeks, Fredrik and I returned home again, troubled by our experiences. Our stay at the monastery in Nepal was much shorter than planned, and I felt that I had failed.

―

> My heart says of you, "Seek his face!"
> Your face, Lord, I will seek.
> —Psalm 27:8

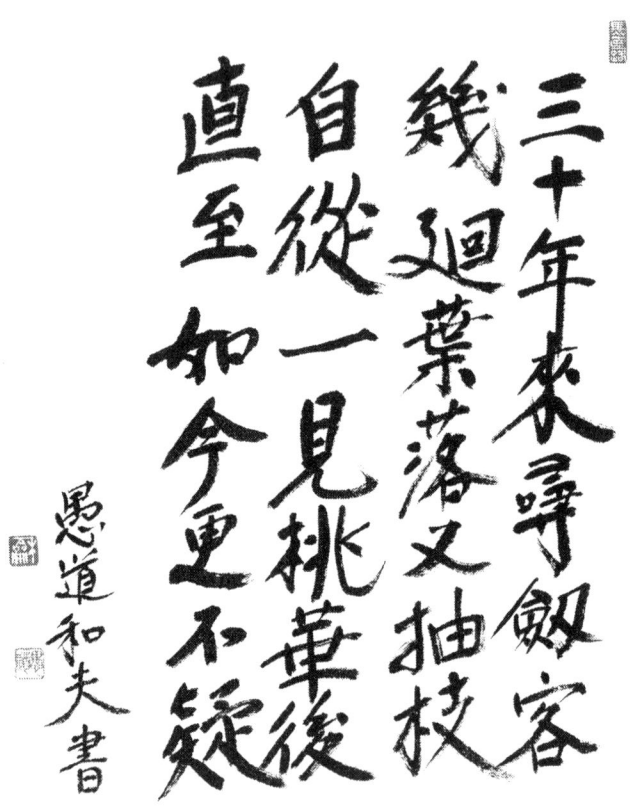

*After one look at the peach blossoms,
I have arrived directly at the present and have no further doubts.*

## Chapter Two

## One Look at the Peach Blossoms

*Monday, April 23, 2012*
I'm walking through a big wooden *torii* gate into the forest surrounding Meiji Shrine in Tokyo. In the middle of this enormous city, I enjoy being among trees and leaves. It's a rainy day, and on the smaller roads, it's just the ravens and me. The torii gates belong to the old, traditional Shinto religion in Japan. Their symbolic meaning is to remind us that we're entering sacred space. In the Shinto tradition, nature is sacred space.

~

When Fredrik and I were in Kathmandu, the owner of a small bookshop had recommended to me a book by the Vietnamese Zen (Thien) Buddhist monk Thich Nhat Hanh. It was a biography of Buddha Shakyamuni's life and teachings. I bought the book from the old man, and it touched me deeply. In November the following year, my friend Johannes and I went for a one-week retreat in Plum Village, Nhat Hanh's monastery near Bordeaux in southwestern France.

One early morning after sitting meditation in the Upper Hamlet of Plum Village, I stood on a gravel path and looked around. The air was damp, and the sun was rising. I noticed, in a new way, how green the grass really was. It was not that I had any clever idea that solved the puzzle. It was nothing dramatic at all, but the feeling that something was lacking was not there anymore. I felt close to the grass and the gravel path, and even close to people who were far away in time and space. The grass was just so green and complete.

The second half of the poem from Dogen Zenji's "Keiseisanshiki" continues:

> After one look at the peach blossoms,
> I have arrived directly at the present and have no further doubts.

I grew up with a dog, a Welsh springer spaniel. His name was Tasse, and he was a good friend. When we went for walks, I used to tell him about my ideas and how I was trying to understand life. He must have been bored with all my self-centered talk, but he was a patient listener. One late summer evening when I was about twenty-one years old, Tasse and I went for a walk. At the top of a hill where we had a view of the city lights in the valley below, we stopped and stood for some time. Tasse sniffed around a birch tree, and I looked at the green leaves. Somehow it struck me that I couldn't really touch or catch the leaves with my thoughts, no matter how clever I tried to be. Not even the smallest leaf right in front of me. My ideas collapsed like a house of cards.

At first, it was difficult for me to let go of the sense of control that my systematic existential and religious ideas had given me. But the leaves broke through and revealed that life's fullness can't be caught in a theory or combination of words, no matter how beautiful and correct they are. God can't be preserved in any tin can of words. Life doesn't depend on my trying to figure it out; it's given moment by moment. The concepts of understanding and not understanding fell away, and the leaves opened themselves. No separation. It was mercy, grace, and a wonderful relief.

No longer was God something that I struggled to reach and achieve with my thoughts; God, to me, became being itself, not confined to the concepts of understanding and not understanding. And I'm already here, in God, as I am. I noticed that I no longer had the feeling of wanting to punch God out of anger and frustration; I felt grateful and embraced.

I continued to have similar experiences now and then. Though these experiences didn't make me different from anyone else, something stayed with me and something changed in me. They helped me see that I needed something more than ideas and that I needed to practice stopping and being still, to look and listen, to let go and receive. I needed to stop, not only to rest, but to be more directly in life as it is; not to turn away, but to turn back to this moment and experience connection and wholeness. This, to me, is meditation, and I continued to practice it at home and at Zen Buddhist retreats.

In the Zen tradition, there is a story about a woman who points her finger at the moon to show her friend where it is in the sky, but her friend only looks at her finger and doesn't see the moon. With help from meditation, I came to regard words, thoughts, and images more like that. They are important and unavoidable, but if I only look at the words, I won't see the moon, because the pointing finger can never be the moon itself.

In my experience, to practice coming back with my whole being to life right now is like passing through a torii gate. I think this place is sacred. It's the moon, and it's the realm of God.

But ask the animals, and they will teach you,
or the birds in the sky, and they will tell you;
or speak to the earth, and it will teach you,
or let the fish in the sea inform you.
—Job 12:7–8

*Naked mind at the present moment.*

## *Chapter Three*
# Naked Mind at the Present Moment

*Tuesday, April 24, 2012*
My friend Peter Rocca and I are looking for an Indian restaurant in the Ueno area of Tokyo. Peter is a Zen Buddhist teacher and an ordained monk, and we studied and trained with the same Zen master here in Japan. We found a small curry house earlier, but they had no vegetarian food, so we're looking for another place. Street after street, and the rain is pouring down on us. After a long walk in Ueno, we take the Yamanote railway line to the Shibuya district of Tokyo and, not too wet from the rain, finally sit down with vegetarian curry. We share and listen to each other's experiences of Christianity and

Buddhism. It's a pleasure to spend time with Peter again.

⁓

Our Zen teacher, Gudo Wafu Nishijima Roshi, was born 1919 in Yokohama, Japan. His father worked for the Furukawa Electric Wire Company and later on for a company that made rubber products. He had four sisters and one brother, but his brother and one of his sisters died when they were infants. Nishijima told me that his mother and father loved their children very much.

As a young boy, Nishijima felt weak and depressed. His father wanted to help and asked him to run a certain distance in the street every evening. Nishijima followed his father's advice, and little by little, the distance got longer. With time he felt better, and he continued doing physical training regularly throughout his life.

When Nishijima was sixteen years old, he was concerned about the violence between right- and left-wing political movements and the economic difficulties in Japan. With a troubled mind regarding what side he should choose, he went to his first Zen meditation retreat, called *sesshin* in Japanese, at a temple called Daichuji near Tokyo. The teacher at the retreat was Kodo Sawaki Roshi, and Nishijima was impressed with his teachings of a balanced middle way.

Kodo Sawaki was a Japanese Soto Zen Buddhist monk who emphasized the importance of sitting meditation, or *zazen* in Japanese. He spent many years of his life traveling around Japan to give lectures and lead sesshin. Because he had no temple of his own, he was sometimes called Homeless Kodo. After the retreat, Nishijima continued studying Buddhism, practicing zazen on a daily basis, and going to retreats as often as he could. He found meditation to be similar to physical training; for him, zazen was the most reliable way to keep a balanced state of body and mind.

In the spring of 1943, Nishijima was drafted by the Japanese army to become a soldier in World War II. Japan had invaded Manchuria in the northeast part of China, and it was the duty of all young Japanese men to join the military. After a few months of training in Japan, Nishijima's group was sent to a Japanese military city in the northwest district of Manchuria called Songo. It was cold in Songo, and their military training continued. They carried bags, ran in the fields, and shot their guns. There was no fighting in the area at the time, and Nishijima's group guarded the district.

Toward the end of the war, the military group that Nishijima belonged to was sent to fight on Leyte Island in Southeast Asia. Because Nishijima had received special training in Songo, he was separated from the group and sent on dangerous roads through Korea and back to Japan to help defend the Japanese mainland against an invasion. No one from his group survived the war on the islands in Southeast Asia.

Nishijima was in the city of Himeji in August 1945 when the war ended. In September, he was allowed to go back home. On his way home, he saw that almost all the big train stations had been completely destroyed. "After the bombings," he said, "Tokyo was almost like a field without any houses."

While Nishijima was in Manchuria, his father died. His mother was sick when he got home, and she died one month later. For several months, Nishijima stayed with his older sister in Tokyo. It was difficult to find food, and they often had to travel far to buy vegetables and grains. Food prices had increased enormously, and money was not very valuable. To get food, they had to trade clothes and other things from their home with the farmers. Sometimes Nishijima traveled to the nearby city of Chiba to buy fish, which he brought back and sold in Tokyo.

Before being drafted, Nishijima had enrolled as a law student in Tokyo. After the war, he completed his studies and became one of the last graduates of Tokyo Imperial University; later the name was changed to Tokyo University. He then worked at a department of the Japanese Ministry of Finance for many years.

Nishijima met and married his wife, and they had a daughter. While living family life, he continued practicing zazen every day and going to Buddhist lectures and retreats as often as he could. When he was fifty-three years old, he was ordained as a monk by Rempo Niwa Zenji, who was the seventy-seventh abbot of the Soto Zen head temple, Eiheiji. As a monk, Nishijima remained married, which is common in Japan. He was also a devoted reader and translator of the Shobogenzo by the thirteenth-century monk Dogen Zenji.

In 1977, Nishijima received dharma transmission, called *shiho* in Japanese, from Rempo Niwa. In short, the Sanskrit word *dharma* means the nature of reality, and it can also refer to the teachings of the Buddha. Nishijima explained that shiho is a traditional ceremony through which a teacher gives his or her mature student a formal certification to be a teacher. After receiving shiho from Rempo Niwa, Nishijima published several books in Japanese and in English, led retreats, and gave lectures in Japan and abroad on Buddhist practice and teachings.

About ten years after receiving dharma transmission, Nishijima worked for the Ida Ryogokudo Company in Tokyo. The company owned a building with four floors in Ichikawa, near Tokyo. It was originally built for employees during a time when housing was difficult to find, but in 1987, the housing situation had improved. The company transformed the building into a Zen practice and retreat center, with Nishijima as the resident teacher. He named it the Dogen Sangha Zazen Dojo.

On the ground floor were a kitchen and a dining room, a library, and a bathroom. On the second floor, there were two large rooms with floors made of tatami straw mats, one for sitting and walking meditation, called *zendo* in Japanese, and one for lectures that were called dharma talks. The remaining two floors were private rooms for the residents. Nishijima welcomed anyone who was interested in practicing zazen, regardless of gender, nationality, or religion.

The first period of sitting meditation in the dojo was from five thirty to six fifteen in the morning. Afterward, Nishijima stood outside the entrance to the zendo and said, "Good morning," in Japanese or English to everyone before the residents went downstairs to eat breakfast together. The meals, and the cleaning up afterward, were mostly silent.

There were four scheduled periods of zazen every day, and the residents shared responsibilities for cooking and cleaning. Some of the residents went to work on weekdays, but there was a minimum requirement to do zazen at least two times a day. Usually, everyone sat together again for the last scheduled zazen period at nine o'clock in the evening. On weekends, there were often dharma talks and more zazen. Nishijima was also available for private meetings related to the practice. The door was always open to the dojo, and its purpose was to help combine meditation training with everyday life.

I met Nishijima for the first time in February 2001 at his office in Tokyo. He was eighty-one years old, and the Ida Ryogokudo business card he gave me said, "Advisory Priest." I was a twenty-two-year-old theology student from Umeå University traveling around in Japan, looking for a Zen teacher, and Nishijima was interested in learning more about Christianity. At the time, he was even studying Biblical Hebrew because of his interest in Judaism and Christianity. We talked for hours, and I was especially touched by his emphasis that zazen isn't only for monks and nuns. The only requirement is to be a human being.

Nishijima told me that when he was about six years old, he attended a church service with one of his sisters. He did not understand much of what the priest said, but he heard something about God in heaven. After the service, he wondered where heaven was, and he could not let go of the idea of God. For many years, he pondered the question until he arrived at a conclusion:

> When I am standing on the earth, I feel that the earth really exists. And when I feel warm in the sunshine, it is completely impossible

for me to doubt the real existence of the sun. Therefore, I feel that we are living in the gorgeous and mysterious universe, and we can think that we are always living in God. Arriving at the conclusion that I am living in God, I feel very peaceful.

After our first meeting, I wanted to keep in touch and learn more from Nishijima. He became my Zen teacher, and over the following years, I continued to train and study with him in the dojo as often as I could. Sometimes I stayed for weeks and sometimes for months. In between my retreats in Japan, we continued our dialogue by writing letters and e-mails to each other.

Nishijima gave dharma transmission to some of his students, and in the beginning of 2004, he offered it to me. I hesitated because I felt more Christian than Buddhist, and I didn't think I was qualified to be a teacher. He said to me that zazen is practical and doesn't rely on any religious creed. "So, you like both Christianity and Buddhism?" he said. "There is no problem."

In the summer of 2004, I lived in the dojo while taking summer courses at the UN University in Tokyo. Zen meditation was a central part of my life, but I still had doubts whether I should go through with the shiho ceremony or not. My classmates at the university, as well as my friends in the dojo, came from many different countries and religious backgrounds. Our connection and friendship across traditions and cultures helped me decide to accept Nishijima's offer.

At the end of June 2004, Nishijima held the *jukai* ceremony for me, before I could receive shiho from him. During jukai the student receives the Buddhist precepts. They vary a bit between different traditions but usually include refraining from intoxicants, killing, stealing, harmful speech, and harmful sexual behavior. Nishijima said that the precepts are like a fence around a wide meadow, and we're like cows in that meadow. We can play freely within the safety of the fence, but outside of it are dangerous situations.

The precepts I received also included not to brag about myself or talk badly about others, not to become angry, and not to desire too much. I appreciated, for example, that it didn't say that I shouldn't have any desire at all. It seems to me that this version of the precept recognizes that to have some desire is a natural part of being human, but it is excessive desire that causes harm. I think it's an example of Nishijima's balanced and humanistic approach to Zen practice.

In a sense, receiving the jukai precepts means living with continuous mistakes, but I don't think the purpose is about weighing me down with failure. Rather, the purpose is to provide me with a sense of direction, over and over again. A ship on the ocean needs the stars for direction and safety, especially at night. But it doesn't mean that the ship is always able to travel on a straight path or that it will one day arrive at the perfect, idealistic destination. In real life, the ship meets winds, waves, and currents on the ocean and does its best to navigate accordingly. I take wrong turns, make mistakes, and get lost, but the stars remain in the sky to help me find direction and a safe shore, over and over again.

In the jukai ceremony, the student receives a *rakusu* with a personal dharma name. A rakusu is a rectangular piece of cloth sewn with a certain pattern and is worn hanging from the neck. Usually the rakusu is sewn by the recipient, but there was not enough time for me to do the sewing before the date Nishijima had set for the ceremony. At the time, there was a Japanese man living in the dojo who had a mental health condition. One of his therapeutic practices had been to sew a rakusu. The stitches were far from perfect, but he kindly gave it to me.

On the back of the dark blue rakusu was a square of white cloth where Nishijima wrote a dharma name in Japanese calligraphy for me: Ryuei Kakudo. He said that Ryuei means "great dragon" and Kakudo means "realizing the way" or "the way of realization." I was a bit embarrassed by the meaning of the name because I don't think of myself as a great dragon who is realizing the way. But I think it was one of Nishijima's ways of supporting and encouraging me. I have never really used the name for anything, but it's part of my life. The rakusu, with all of its messy stitches, is beautiful to me.

In early July, Nishijima held the shiho ceremony for one of his Japanese students and me. During the ceremony, he gave us several traditional items, among them a set of eating bowls called *oryoki*, a dharma transmission certificate written on a large piece of cloth, and a robe called *kesa* (Japanese) or *kashaya* (Sanskrit).

I also received two wooden sticks, one long called *shippei* and one short called *kotsu* or *nyoi*. The kotsu is about as long as my forearm, with carved patterns in the dark wood. The stick is slightly curved, similar to a human spine. One end is wrapped with a cord, like a handle, with a tassel hanging at the end. As far as I understand, the kotsu is a sign of approval that a Zen teacher gives to his or her student who has been given permission to teach. During his dharma talks, Nishijima often held his kotsu, which Rempo Niwa had given him.

The long shippei is red and black and also made from wood. I never saw it being used for anything in the dojo. It looks somewhat like a sword, and the airport staff wouldn't allow me to bring it along as carry-on luggage on the flight back home. Now it hangs on a wall in one of our closets in Umeå, and I'm not sure what to say to our kids when they find it.

For me to receive shiho from Nishijima under these circumstances was unconventional, as Nishijima often was. I had not lived for years in a traditional Soto Zen training monastery, I had not learned how to perform Buddhist ceremonies, and I was a young and relatively inexperienced Christian man from Sweden. In more than one sense, I didn't deserve it at all. But I chose to trust in Nishijima's trust in me. It gave me the confidence I needed to start leading zazen groups and arranging meditation retreats in and around my hometown in Sweden. I'm very grateful to Nishijima for his generous support and unconventional trust in me, but I'm afraid that I'm embodying the traditional role of a Zen teacher quite poorly.

Nishijima's wife became ill and died in 2005, and he had problems with his own health. He could no longer lead the dojo, and the company closed it down. The building was demolished, and the area made into a parking lot. Nishijima retired and moved to an apartment in Takashimadaira, in the northwest part of Tokyo. He bought two extra beds and invited his students to visit him in his home, which he regarded as the new zazen dojo. I visited and stayed with Nishijima several times in his apartment, for one or two weeks at a time. We cooked, ate, and washed dishes together. We went for long walks, and we practiced zazen together, sitting in his small living room. And we continued to have many talks on Christianity, Buddhism, and zazen.

After sitting meditation and breakfast, we often went for a walk together, and then I usually left the apartment for a while during the day to give us both some space. One day, during a visit in 2007, I was meeting friends in Tokyo and took the train back to Takashimadaira at about six o'clock in the evening. When I walked from the train station back to the apartment complex where Nishijima lived, a police officer on a bicycle stopped me politely. I couldn't understand what he was saying in Japanese, but I heard him say something that sounded like my last name, and then something about Nishijima-san.

During the day, Nishijima had become worried about me. I don't know why, but he thought that I might be lost in Tokyo and couldn't find my way back to his apartment. He had called the police. The kind police officer, with his bicycle, accompanied me to the building where Nishijima lived. Nishijima was happy and relieved when he opened the door, and he had prepared a special traditional vegetarian dinner to celebrate that I had returned safely.

With time, Nishijima's condition became worse. The last time I saw him was when I stayed with him in his apartment in 2008. From what I have heard, his daughter took care of him, and he was in a hospital and a nursing home in his last years. During this time, none of his students was able to contact him. On Tuesday, January 28, 2014, Gudo Nishijima Roshi died at ninety-four years old.

Once, in his apartment, I asked Nishijima if he would like to make a calligraphy painting for me. At first, he politely declined, because he had not practiced calligraphy in a long time and his old hands had become shaky with age. But later on, he asked me what calligraphy I would like him to make. I looked through his English translations of Dogen's books and provided him with a number of suggestions that he could choose from.

A couple of days later, when I returned to the apartment in the afternoon, he had almost finished painting all of my suggestions, and now the calligraphy paintings have become titles for the chapters in this book. In the lower left corner, he wrote his name, Gudo Wafu, and put his signature stamp. In the upper right corner, he put another stamp with characters he translated as, "Spring wind is peaceful and relaxed."

I asked Nishijima which one of my calligraphy suggestions was his favorite, and he answered in Japanese: "Sekishin-henpen." Nishijima explained that *seki* is the color red, and the meaning is naked, honest, and sincere. *Shin* means heart or mind. *Henpen* is every moment, or at the present moment. The naked and sincere mind at the present moment, he said, is more balanced and freer. It's not caught in too much desire. It's not stuck in memories of the past or ideas of the future. Then he laughed and said that there is also more humor in this state of mind.

—

> Above all else, guard your heart,
> for everything you do flows from it.
> —Proverbs 4:23

*Only the act of sitting.*

# Chapter Four
## Only the Act of Sitting

*Wednesday, April 25, 2012*
Today I'm visiting the Zen Buddhist temple Rinsenji in Tokyo. After a friendly welcome, it's time to practice sitting and walking meditation with the residents of the temple and other guests. At Rinsenji the practice is more traditionally strict compared to Nishijima Roshi's dojo. For example, I'm corrected when I step into the zendo with the wrong foot first. I'm corrected again when I turn around in the wrong direction, and I begin to feel a little bit tense. Suddenly, I see someone smiling kindly at me from the other side of the room. A smile can be a miracle. Sometimes it changes everything.

During sitting meditation at Rinsenji, when I make a signal by holding my palms together in front of me, one of the monks walks slowly to my place. We bow, and he hits the back of my shoulders, two times on each side, with a long, flat stick called *kyosaku*. It's meant to be helpful when I'm sleepy or have uncomfortable tensions in my back. Then I breathe in and return to sitting still to do zazen. I breathe out, let go, and let zazen do me.

―

*Zazen* is a Japanese word that is often translated as "sitting meditation." *Za* means "to sit" and *zen* roughly means "meditation." As the word *meditation*, by itself, is a broad term that can be used with several different meanings, I use the more specific word *zazen*. This practice is also called *shikantaza* in Japanese. Nishijima explained that *shikan* means "only," *ta* indicates action, to do something, and *za* is "to sit." Literally, *shikantaza* means "only the act of sitting."

The Japanese word *zen* is derived from the Chinese word *chan*, which in turn comes from the Sanskrit word *dhyana*. All of these words mean "meditation" or "meditative state," but not in the sense of pondering. Nishijima said that zazen is shikantaza. "Just do it," he said, "and don't worry about ideas or goals." There is no idealistic goal to strive for. It's not about gaining something new, deep, or hidden; it's returning to just this place and this moment as it is.

Nishijima didn't use a kyosaku stick. He said that it's better to learn to wake up by ourselves. Neither did he focus much on how to step into the zendo. His emphasis was on practicing zazen every day and bringing that balance into daily life.

Zazen is based on a posture that is comfortable, firm, upright, balanced, and still. The purpose of this posture is to help both body and mind to be more relaxed and stable, more awake and balanced, and more at peace.

Zen practitioners usually sit on a round cushion called a *zafu* that is large enough for the body to be comfortable. A kneeling bench can also be used. Feet and legs rest on something soft on the floor, such as a flat cushion called a *zabuton*, a folded blanket, a thick mat, or grass if meditating outdoors. In order to create a comfortable and calm environment for all the senses, wearing loose clothing in subdued colors is recommended, and it's better to not use strong perfumes and to keep the body and clothes clean.

To make a firm base is fundamental to the practice. In the kneeling posture, called *seiza*, the lower legs are folded under the thighs, with the knees in front resting on the ground and kept a bit apart for stability. The ankles are flat on the ground. If the ankles hurt, a rolled-up blanket or something similar can be put under them to create a more comfortable angle for the feet.

In the lotus or Burmese postures, the legs are folded with the knees to the sides. You can choose to have one or both ankles on the ground, or on the opposite calf or thigh. Both ankles on the ground makes the so-called Burmese posture. One foot on the opposite calf is called quarter lotus. One foot on the opposite thigh is a half lotus and putting both feet on the opposite thighs makes the full lotus posture. For stability, it's important that both knees rest firmly on the ground; if necessary, you can put a small cushion under one or both knees.

Sometimes I enjoy sitting in the seiza posture, but I usually sit with my legs folded with my knees to the sides. After about twenty years of practice, my legs are still quite stiff, and most often I sit with both ankles on the ground, one in front of the other.

The head, neck, and spine are kept in a relaxed, upright position without leaning against anything or to either side. It can be helpful to first stretch the top of the head as high up toward the sky as possible, and then relax into a comfortable upright posture. It's also helpful to rock the upper body slowly a little bit—front and back and side to side—until you find the balance point in which the spine rests as much as possible on itself. Keep the pelvis slightly tilted forward, but not too much.

Sit silent and still and let the movement of the breathing flow naturally and sink down into the abdomen by itself. With relaxed shoulders, let the hands rest joined together in the lap. One hand rests in the other, with one thumb over the other. Or gently hold the tips of the thumbs against each other, forming an oval shape, which is the traditional way to hold the hands during zazen in the Soto Zen tradition. Letting the hands rest joined together in the lap can give you a sense of focus and unity and help the shoulders relax without slouching. It can also help the spine to stay aligned, without leaning on anything.

When you feel sleepy, you can open the eyes wide for a while, and when you need to calm down, you can close the eyes for a while. But in general, keep the mouth closed and eyes open in a relaxed way, and rest your gaze on the ground or the lower part of a wall about a meter or two in front of you. Avoid keeping the eyes closed because you can become sleepy and drift off into dreams. Zazen isn't about sleeping, escaping, or closing our eyes to ourselves or to the world; it's about being present and paying attention to what is here and now, in and around us.

These are practical guidelines for finding a comfortable and solid upright posture, but they are not to be regarded as strict laws. I find these sitting postures, along with being in firm contact with the ground, to be helpful, but it's not some kind of prestigious accomplishment. If necessary, you can use a chair, lie down, or find some other way that works for you. Our bodies and the condition of our health are different and changing. Use the posture that suits you best.

It's possible to do sitting meditation almost anywhere, but if possible, a calm and comfortable place is recommended. Don't sit in complete darkness because, just like closing the eyes, it can make you sleepy. In order to keep warm and to help with blood circulation, you can, if you like, put a large blanket around the legs and shoulders. Avoid practicing zazen when too tired, too hungry, or too full and drowsy just after eating a meal.

I like to do zazen outdoors. Maybe it's the oxygen that makes me more alert, but there is something about sitting in nature. After an outdoor retreat, my friend Mats said, "Sometimes warm, sometimes cold—it's like life itself."

Indoors, it's common to sit facing a wall, about a meter or two in front of it, in order to minimize distractions. But in a church, meditators usually sit facing the altar. Outdoors, you can sit facing an open space, such as a lake or a field. But pretty much anywhere is fine.

In the zendo, cushions and mats are laid in straight lines and the room is kept simple and clean, with only a few decorations: a flower, a couple of candles, maybe a piece of wood or some rocks, or perhaps a calligraphy painting or something else that is inspirational. In a Christian context, an icon or a cross could be displayed. In order to maintain a calm atmosphere, books, texts, or other things that trigger intellectual and analytical thoughts are not kept in the zendo, and too much color and decoration is also avoided.

Sometimes other people may walk or drive by you while you are doing sitting or walking meditation. I like to think that meditation practice, just like other states of mind, can be contagious. Maybe someone who passes by and happens to see you slows down a little bit and by doing so returns to more awareness of life in this present moment.

I have heard it said that zazen in a Christian church is different from zazen in a Buddhist temple. But in zazen we practice letting go of only looking at the pointing fingers, and we sit with the moon itself. We sit with breath, spine, and legs and with our whole heart of flesh and blood, regardless of whether we do zazen in a church, a temple, or our backyard.

In Nishijima's dojo, I remember a man who had difficulties sitting still and who changed his posture often. Sometimes he sighed loudly and completely gave up sitting upright, but he stayed on the cushion until the sound of the ending bell. I never heard Nishijima say one critical word about it, but I do remember once during breakfast Nishijima complimenting him on his efforts and saying that he was doing well, within hearing of everyone at the table.

It does take some effort to get used to sitting still, and that is part of the practice. But if you experience pain, you are free to calmly and quietly stretch out or change your posture. When my leg falls asleep in the Burmese posture, for example, I gently shift the position of my feet and put the inside foot in front of the other. Or if I'm in the seiza posture, I may slowly rise up on my knees for a little while. Usually that is enough, and my legs are comfortable again.

Once during zazen at an outdoor retreat, an ant climbed up onto my right foot and got inside the leg of my pants. To climb onto my foot was OK, and I remained still, but I didn't let him get very far up my leg before I helped him down to the ground again. We can keep a similar approach to physical discomfort and pain. Sometimes when I lead a period of zazen together with beginners, I make sure to change my own posture a little bit early on to help others relax and feel free to do the same.

When a mosquito bite itches, either do or don't scratch it. But do not think or worry about whether you should scratch it or not. In general, Nishijima taught that we don't have to worry about these things at all. Scratch the bite or let it be, and return to shikantaza, just sitting still, again.

Meditation is not a competition of any sort. It's not about being better than anyone else. We're not better at meditation if we can sit still for a long time, and we're not worse if we can sit still only for a short time. The concepts of better and worse don't really apply: find a balanced way to enjoy the practice.

If possible, sit in a quiet place, but a little bit of sound is no problem. Even though we sit silent and still, sometimes there are sounds from breathing or coughing, from swallowing saliva, or from the stomach. When I was nineteen years old and had just started doing zazen with a group in Umeå, I was hard on myself and worried that my body would make sounds that would disturb others in the group. Now I know that I was probably only disturbing myself. Try to be as quiet and still as possible during zazen, but you are also free to relax. A little sound is no problem.

For several months, there was a construction site outside the yoga studio where we used to practice zazen together in Umeå. Suddenly, during Friday morning meditation, the sharp sound of a big hammer drill cut through the silence, and the whole building was shaking like it was an earthquake. It was quite a comical situation, but it was also an opportunity for training and exploration of meditation in a new situation. Actually, it was more difficult when I could hear the workers talk with one another, because it gave rise to chains of thought that made me drift off in a way that the hammer drill did not.

I enjoy doing zazen and arranging retreats outdoors where there are many different sounds from the wind, birds, waves, trees, rain, and so on. I find it nourishing to sit among these sounds and movements in nature. The training is to stay still with posture and breathing and to pay attention. When a bird sings or a dog barks, we let it fill our whole being, and then we practice letting it go. When we suddenly hear a voice, a cell phone, or a bus driving by, if we like, we can put a label on it—voice, cell phone, bus—in order to help us let it go and to continue only sitting still right here in this place. Also, putting a smile on our lips sometimes makes it easier to let go; I noticed that it worked especially well with the noise from the hammer drill.

When Nishijima was asked about whether or not we can listen to music during zazen, he smiled and said, "Perhaps silence is best." Listening to music can be a wonderful healing experience, but during zazen it can make us more easily drift off into dreams and emotions. I think zazen can be described as listening to the silence that heals.

Once during a period of group meditation in Umeå, a man suddenly fell down on the floor. My friend Daniel and I quickly went over to check on how he was doing. We were about to call an ambulance, when the man explained that he faints sometimes, and it was nothing unusual. We helped him over to a couch where he lay down and rested while we continued our meditation training with the group. After we had finished the last period of zazen, he felt better and joined us for a cup of tea. I was impressed with how the whole group held the situation with a calm and compassionate silence, firmly rooted in the energy of the practice.

Before sitting down and before getting up from zazen, we hold our palms together with the fingertips somewhere a bit in front of the nose and bow gently in a gesture called *gassho* in Japanese. It's both an expression and a practice of being grateful for the life that we share in this moment and for the privilege to have an opportunity to do zazen.

Meditation begins at a zendo by bowing when entering the room, choosing a place, bowing again, and establishing a sitting posture. Then I usually enjoy taking a few deep breaths. The meditator then listens to three chimes of a bell—each chime almost ringing out before the next one begins. Sometimes I just listen to the sound and let it call me to meditation, and sometimes I enjoy a simple form of prayer with the three sounds of the bell.

With the first sound, I pray for peace and well-being in myself; with the second sound, for my family, relatives, and friends. And with the third sound, for all living beings, including those I find difficult to wish well. During the first chime, I breathe in while saying, "Peace," silently in my mind, and breathe out, "in me." During the second chime, I breathe in, "Peace," and breathe out, "for family and friends." And during the third chime, I breathe in, "Peace," and breathe out, "for all living beings." It's a simple prayer and training in wishing all beings well, inspired by a Buddhist practice called *metta* or lovingkindness meditation. It is available at any time and not only at the beginning of zazen.

When a group sits regularly together for meditation, the participants can decide, if they like, to alternate who is responsible for ringing the bell in order to prevent prestige from finding its way into the group. I think it's important that the participants are free to draw upon one another's experiences and share suitable responsibilities among themselves in the practice community.

After the three chimes of the bell, a great silence opens. The stillness lets us notice more clearly what we carry within us. At this point, it's easy to become disappointed with meditation, because what is moving within you might be quite different from your idealistic expectations of what meditation should be. Zazen can be calm and easy to enjoy, but sometimes it's like sitting in a storm, or it's just incredibly boring. One is not better or more valuable than the other; they are different sides of the same zazen.

There is a funny and important story about a monk in a monastery who is learning about meditation. After some time, he goes to the abbot and complains about meditation being difficult in several ways. The abbot smiles and calmly replies that this is normal and will pass and recommends that the monk continue with the practice. Some months later on, the monk returns to the abbot, excited to tell him that his meditation feels great and is going very well. Once again, the abbot smiles, tells him that this is normal and will pass and recommends that the monk continue with the practice.

In zazen, we practice non-thinking by letting everything come as it is and letting everything go as it is, without analysis and categorization. We practice receiving and letting go of thoughts, images, and emotions; we don't fight with them. We don't try to push down the waves, because it will only create more waves and tensions in us. With time, the waves will usually calm down by themselves, and a deeper silence will prevail.

Sometimes you may notice that you have drifted far off. But when dreams, emotions, and chains of thought pull you away, it doesn't mean that you have failed or that your meditation is bad. Actually, every time you find that you have drifted off, it means that your practice is working well because you have noticed it. Then you have a chance to return to this place, to enjoy the posture and the breathing. We return to doing, as a way of letting go of thinking. We begin anew, again and again. It's a central and inescapable part of the training.

Nishijima said that zazen can be like taking the lid off a boiling pot. Letting the bubbles of steam come just as they are is a way to release tensions from the body and mind, but we need to be careful when there are big bubbles of hot steam.

When difficult waves of thoughts and emotions arise within me, I practice receiving and holding them just like we held our newborn children when they woke up at night. We held them with loving care, patiently keeping them closely embraced until they stopped crying. Then, when they had calmed down and fallen asleep, we lay them down in their bed again. In a similar way, we can practice both receiving and letting go of difficult waves with loving care.

We can use awareness of our upright sitting posture and our breathing as a way to hold steady during the storm. For example, we can notice the sensations in the body when we breathe in and out: how the air flows through the nose, how it fills the lungs, and how the belly and chest move up and down. We pay attention to the breaths just as they are and let them calm down by themselves.

There are visualizations that have been helpful to me sometimes when big, difficult waves arise. For example, I imagine sitting solid like a mountain and open like the sky, through all the different weathers that appear in me and around me. Or I sit like a heavy stone that has sunk to the bottom of a river and is resting completely still, letting all the water flow by it. Or I sit like a duck that is floating on the surface of the ocean, as the waves rise and fall. Sometimes a big wave rolls over me and tumbles me around before I'm able to rest on the surface again.

I used to think that a balanced, solid meditation always meant being like a mountain or a heavy stone on the bottom of a river, but I found that it also entails being open like the sky and riding the waves like a duck. Sometimes it means laughing with joy or crying with grief, without hesitation. Always it means being kind to myself through it all.

It happens sometimes that we have strange experiences during sitting meditation. When it happens to me, it's usually when I'm tired or sleepy. For example, I can feel light or heavy or see waves or changes in the light. This is called *makyo* in Japanese, and it's not something to either worry about or be excited about. We accept it, usually sit through it, and then we let it go.

But if you feel dizzy or in any way unwell, it's important to take a break and rest. I don't think zazen is useful for all conditions of body and mind, and meditation is not a substitute for taking good care of ourselves in other wholesome ways. If you are living with a physical or mental condition, you should consult a physician or a psychiatrist, as well as a meditation teacher, before beginning or continuing with meditation practice.

I once asked Nishijima the age-old existential question that I was invited to look into at Kopan monastery in Nepal: "Who am I?" He answered, "I think it's impossible to know. I'm something ineffable." Then he laughed, knocked gently on his head, and said, "When I want to know who I am, I knock like this on my head. It's a little painful. So, I am."

Nishijima's approach was liberating and refreshing to me. In my experience, letting go of trying to intellectually understand and define who I am has somehow helped me to a sense of who I am. Meditation can help us realize that our identity isn't limited or locked to the ever-changing thoughts and emotions within us, including our ideas of separateness and self.

Dogen Zenji wrote in "Genjo-koan" in the Shobogenzo:

> To learn Buddhism is to learn ourselves. To learn ourselves is to forget ourselves. To forget ourselves is to be experienced by millions of things and phenomena. To be experienced by millions of things and phenomena is to let our own body and mind, and the body and mind of the external world, fall

away. [Then] we can forget the [mental] trace of realization, and show the [real] signs of forgotten realization continually, moment by moment.

I have heard meditation being criticized for being selfish or some kind of self-indulgence, and I see how it can be perceived that way from a distance. But training in giving this moment our complete presence means practicing love for the weaving of all things. It's one of the most valuable gifts we can give one another.

Zazen helps me be freer, right in the middle of ten thousand things, and able to build a home on a foundation more solid than my ideas of myself. It opens up space for me to touch that we're truly here together and that my self is much more, and less, than me.

At one point during the Eucharist service in the Church of Sweden, we all say together that though we're many, we're one body, for we all share one bread (1 Cor. 10:17). My joy and pain are also in you, and yours in me. In my experience, this sense of interconnected identity is nourished by meditation, and it opens up the birthplace for compassion in the heart.

After Jesus Christ had been beaten, tortured, and nailed to a wooden cross, he cried out to God in a loud voice, just before he died, "Father, into your hands I commit my spirit" (Luke 23:46). My colleague and mentor Anders Dahlqvist has been a hospital priest and meditation practitioner for more than twenty years, and he has described meditation as a way of practicing dying. It's training to surrender and let go and entrust oneself into God's hands. It's practicing dying from our ideas of a separate self, and therefore it's also practicing love.

Dogen described zazen as dropping off body and mind ("Bendowa" in the Shobogenzo). I sit still, breathe in, and embrace my whole being with loving care. I breathe out and let go of my whole being with loving care. I just sit, shikantaza, and surrender body and mind in God. Simply continuing with this practice is a goal in itself.

In the dojo, we did zazen for forty-five minutes at a time, except for the last period in the evening, when we sat for thirty minutes. I asked Nishijima several times how long I should sit at home, and he always replied that we're completely free to decide for ourselves. He refused to say any number of minutes. Nishijima emphasized the importance of practicing every day, but I have noticed that if we have too much ambition, we tend to give up after a while. Ambition is a tricky thing when it comes to meditation. Therefore, in the beginning, it was helpful to me to make a commitment to myself just to sit down on the cushion every day, regardless of how long I would stay on it. Just to let my sitting bones touch the cushion was enough. This low level of ambition made it easier for me in everyday life to actually sit down. Then, when I was on the cushion, I could decide how long I would stay there and set a time for myself. And with time it became a habit that I enjoyed.

In my first years of practice, when my mind got bored and restless during zazen, I started looking for interesting thoughts and fantasies in my head that I could use to escape from my restlessness. Sometimes I looked for patterns and counted dots on the floor and wall in front of me. I even tried to calculate how many breaths there were left until the ending bell would set me free, and then I counted down. I believe reactions like these, however silly they may seem, are a common and normal part of the training.

I continued to notice my impulses and reactions, and I continued to return to my posture and breathing, and with time it slowly changed. I still get bored and restless and find myself in fantasies from time to time, but I'm more comfortable with being bored and restless now. I don't feel the same need to escape from it anymore, and I more easily let go of my restlessness. These emotions and I, we're like an old couple. We're life partners, and we're used to being in a silent room together.

At the end of a period of sitting meditation, we listen to one chime of a bell. The three sounds that we listened to in the beginning, sometimes with the threefold prayer, are also one. This ending chime of the bell calls us to bring our meditation training up from the stillness on the cushion and into the movements and meetings of everyday life. Meditation isn't just about ourselves, and we practice helping the chime of the bell reach everywhere, even to the darkest places. Then we bow with joined palms, gently massage feet and legs, and rise carefully from our seats.

When I returned to Plum Village a few years ago, I met one of the senior monks, Brother Phap Kinh, and he kindly helped me in several ways during my one-week retreat. One day at the end of the week, after lunch, there was some free time. I took the opportunity to ask Phap Kinh if he wanted to walk and talk with me. There were some things I wanted to ask him about. He smiled and replied politely that he would like to do that but that he preferred to do one thing wholeheartedly at a time. "We can sit down here or somewhere else and talk, if you like," he said, "or we can take a walk silently together."

When consecutive sessions of zazen are practiced, *kinhin* or walking meditation is often done in between the sitting meditations. After a period of zazen, meditators carefully stand up next to their seats and turn clockwise, usually standing in a square around the perimeter of the room. A chime from a smaller bell or a sound from wooden clappers signals that they are to begin walking around the room in walking meditation.

Kinhin is a way to stretch out the legs between periods of zazen, but it's also a practice on its own. It's training in bringing meditation from stillness into movement. During walking meditation, we're not on our way to somewhere else, but we practice arriving with every careful step—like stepping through the front door of our home after a long journey, over and over again. We practice being aware of how the ground feels beneath our feet. I prefer walking barefoot, but sometimes it is necessary to wear socks or shoes. Our feet move softly, and we try to let our steps flow like waves, anchored in the awareness that the solid ground carries us.

The posture in kinhin is upright and similar to zazen, and the pace is slow enough to take about one or two breaths in and out for every step. Sometimes I synchronize steps and breathing, but most often I enjoy letting it go. If a caterpillar always thought about how and when she moved each leg, it would be impossible for her to crawl. In kinhin, just like in zazen, we practice just doing: only the act of sitting and only the act of walking.

Each step taken in kinhin is about a half to one foot long, and if possible, the meditator walks in a straight line. Traditionally in Soto Zen, the left hand is closed in a fist around the thumb and held with the fingers against the solar plexus, and the other hand is gently covering it, in a posture called *shashu* in Japanese. It can symbolize holding on to a vertical pole for solidity and balance. This posture can help support the shoulders and give a feeling of balance and a sense of unity. But when I do kinhin outdoors and wear a jacket with comfortable pockets, I usually just let my hands rest in my pockets. Just like in zazen, rest your gaze on the ground, a couple of meters in front; when walking outdoors, it's fine to stop sometimes and enjoy looking around.

In between periods of zazen, it's common to do kinhin for about ten or fifteen minutes. But walking meditation can also be done for half an hour or an hour, indoors or outdoors. When in a room with others, meditators walk clockwise around the perimeter, evenly spaced apart. Everyone adopts the same pace as the practice leader. Then, when a chime from a bell or a sound from wooden clappers signals the end of the walking period, the meditators stop briefly, bow, and then continue walking with a faster pace around the room until everyone reaches his or her seat, whereupon everyone bows and sits down for the next period of zazen.

In kinhin, we walk more slowly than usual, but we're also free to adjust the pace according to the situation. Walking meditation isn't only available at retreats or in between periods of sitting; there are many opportunities throughout daily life. It can be done almost anywhere—among the toys lying on our living room floor or in a hospital corridor on the way to visit a friend.

After a group finishes a session of sitting and walking meditation, I like the habit of standing in a circle facing one another, joining the palms together, and, at the sound of a bell or wooden clappers, bowing. I think this way of bowing is also a nice way to start and end a separate period of kinhin together outdoors. I like to do the same when I'm meditating by myself at home.

In August 2013, I began serving as a hospital priest at the University Hospital of Umeå. The ecumenical Hospital Church provides spiritual care to patients and their near and dear ones, and to hospital employees, in the form of, for example, pastoral counseling, crisis support, prayers, and services. On one of my first days, my colleague, hospital pastor Anders Axelsson, told me that walking slowly in the corridors was also an important part of my job.

Sometimes when I'm on my way to a patient, I walk slower than usual and practice walking meditation on the way. It makes me arrive a few minutes later, but I feel more solid when I knock on the door and step into the room. It doesn't make all difficulties go away, but it allows me to be a little more grounded, open, and present with the situation at hand.

In Plum Village, I learned that when big and difficult waves arise during walking meditation, I can visualize releasing them into the earth and making footprints of peace where I walk. I learned that I can do walking meditation side by side or hand in hand with a friend, or even with someone who I'm experiencing difficult feelings with. It's also possible to visualize walking together with anyone, dead or alive. I visualize the two of us releasing our suffering into the ground that carries us both, and we make footprints of peace together on the earth. Then I return to enjoy just walking again.

One summer I got to know a wonderful little boy who was terminally ill with cancer. He died about one month later, and I held his funeral service. I knew it was OK for me to cry a little bit during the service, but at the same time, it was my job to remain calm. When I walked between the small coffin and my seat during the service, I did walking meditation. And when I was sitting down, I kept an upright posture and paid attention to my breathing and followed it with awareness, just as it was. These two simple practices helped me remain grounded, present, and relatively calm in the moment, while at the same time allowing space for the thoughts and emotions that raged in me.

After the funeral service, I had a busy day, and I didn't have time to cry. But during evening zazen the next day, my eyes filled with tears. Thoughts and images of the little boy and his family welled up in me. I was sitting together with others, and although the room was silent, I felt support from the group. I stayed on the cushion with my emotions until the chime from the bell signaled that it was time for walking meditation.

During kinhin that evening, I visualized the boy walking next to me, but in my imagination, he soon became restless and annoyed because I walked so slowly. I couldn't keep from smiling when I thought of him jumping around and pulling my arm to make me come play with him instead of doing that boring kinhin. When I sat down for the next period of zazen, I felt lighter, and I could return to just sitting again.

Jesus often withdrew to lonely places to pray, and he invited us to follow him (Luke 5:16, Mark 6:31). The Japanese word *shin* means both heart and mind, or sometimes center or core, and the word for a Zen meditation retreat, *sesshin*, can be translated as "touching the heart-mind." A sesshin is an opportunity to step away from the ten thousand things and step into a daily schedule of meditation practice together with others.

A sesshin can be done alone, but I find it easier to do with others because of the support from the group. Being together with others is also a part of the training, and it's a way of helping one another. At a sesshin, we have meals and do practical chores together in silence, and we practice meditation in everything we do: brushing teeth, making the bed, and taking a shower or a bath. It's a training camp in just sitting, walking, peeling potatoes, eating silently, and washing dishes together and doing it wholeheartedly, with a whole heart-mind, with awareness in the present moment.

For several years, I spent many months in retreat in Nishijima's dojo and elsewhere. Now my family and work situation is different, and when possible, I like to go to a meditation retreat for about a week once or twice every year. A meditation retreat isn't some kind of competition or achievement, and the purpose isn't to do as many hours of zazen as possible. The purpose is to help our practice become more solid in everyday life.

Nishijima taught that at a sesshin, we wake up a little earlier than usual in the morning, but not too early. It's important to have enough time for sleep. The morning begins with one or two periods of zazen and then breakfast. Nishijima's schedule usually had two forty-five-minute periods of zazen, with kinhin in between, before lunch. A similar block of meditation was also held in the afternoon, followed by one more period of zazen in the evening. Nishijima also gave a daily talk and was available for private meetings, called *dokusan* in Japanese, related to the practice.

Compared to Nishijima's schedule, I believe most sesshin traditions have many more hours of zazen every day, perhaps even double the amount or more, and wake-up time can be as early as two or three hours after midnight. But Nishijima said that a sesshin shouldn't break the balance of ordinary daily life. He said that if we go too far to the left on the road, we fall into the left ditch. And if we go too far to the right on the road, we fall into the right ditch. Nishijima emphasized that zazen isn't an ascetic practice; it's about balance in everyday life. He recommended that we should stay on the road by enjoying a balanced and moderate sesshin schedule.

In June 2014, my friend Daniel and I arranged a one-week outdoor sesshin on an island near Umeå called Stora Fjäderägg. It's a small island, and we had the whole place to ourselves. We had access to cabins where we slept and cooked, but we did zazen, kinhin, meals, and dishwashing outdoors, except one cold morning when the wind was too strong. To arrange a sesshin on the island was a dream come true for me. But a few days into the retreat, I had difficult feelings of doubt. I asked myself, "Why am I here?"

It's a central part of sesshin practice to be with difficult questions and feelings when they arise, because at a meditation retreat, we can't run away. There are no TVs or computers, no phone calls or conversations. There is nowhere to run from this place and this heart-mind. And I think that the opposite of running away is love.

It's not that I'm totally loving and blissful all the time when I come home from a sesshin. It's not like that. Actually, quite the opposite: I'm often a bit tired just after coming home. But in my experience, it's nutrition for the ground, for the soil, from which love can grow. My life isn't just about me. Therefore, through the highs and the lows at retreats, when doubt and difficult feelings come, I try to remind myself sometimes of why we are there: because of love.

The next day on the island, most of the difficult emotions ceased in me, and during zazen in the afternoon, I noticed a small flower next to me. It was weather-beaten and looked like someone had stepped on it—probably me. But it was still opening up to bloom and to receive the sunlight, the air, and the rain. We sat there together, the flower and I. It reminded me that I can't escape, but I'm free to open up to receive this moment and this place and to let the rocks, grass, clouds, and wind touch my heart-mind. We were sitting there, restricted in many ways, the flower and I, and we were free.

By the time Nishijima was eighty-six years old, he had been practicing zazen every day for about seventy years. One morning in his apartment, I asked him how zazen was different from the first time he tried it. He laughed and said, "It's completely the same." I think this open beginner's mind is an important foundation of zazen, because thinking in terms of better or more advanced can make me so stuck in myself that I close my eyes, cover my ears, and lock my heart.

Nishijima continued to say that, at the same time, zazen had always helped him come back to the present moment, as it is, which had been a great source of happiness in his life. "The waves have become smaller," he said, "but big or small waves aren't the problem." Then he laughed again and advised me to enjoy the waves, both big and small.

Just this in-breath and out-breath, in this moment, is the same for beginners and longtime practitioners alike. When I tried to explain this approach at a meditation course that I held for university employees in Umeå, one of the course participants said that I had to work on my marketing skills. But I don't think meditation training should be marketed in the same way that most other things are sold in the world—with promises of bigger, better, and more improved.

Zazen and kinhin is training in sitting and walking defenseless, with the trust, presence, and open eyes of a little child, with a beginner's eyes, open to this eternal and ever-changing whole and new now.

Nishijima taught the importance of daily practice, but he also emphasized the importance of not doing too much zazen. I find it helpful to have a daily meditation routine, but you're free to adapt the practice to your circumstances. For example, when I stayed in Thailand for a while and spent most of my time outdoors, there were many sand fleas in the grass and in the sand that bit me when I sat still on the ground. During those weeks, I mostly did walking meditation instead of sitting.

I usually do sitting or walking meditation at least once or twice every day, and I practice bringing it with me into everything I do. In my experience, with time, daily meditation training becomes a source of habit energy that we can connect with in everyday life. If for some reason we don't do zazen or kinhin one day, then we just continue the next day. There is no problem. We're free to smile, relax, and begin anew.

> Be still before the Lord,
> and wait patiently for him.
> —Psalm 37:7

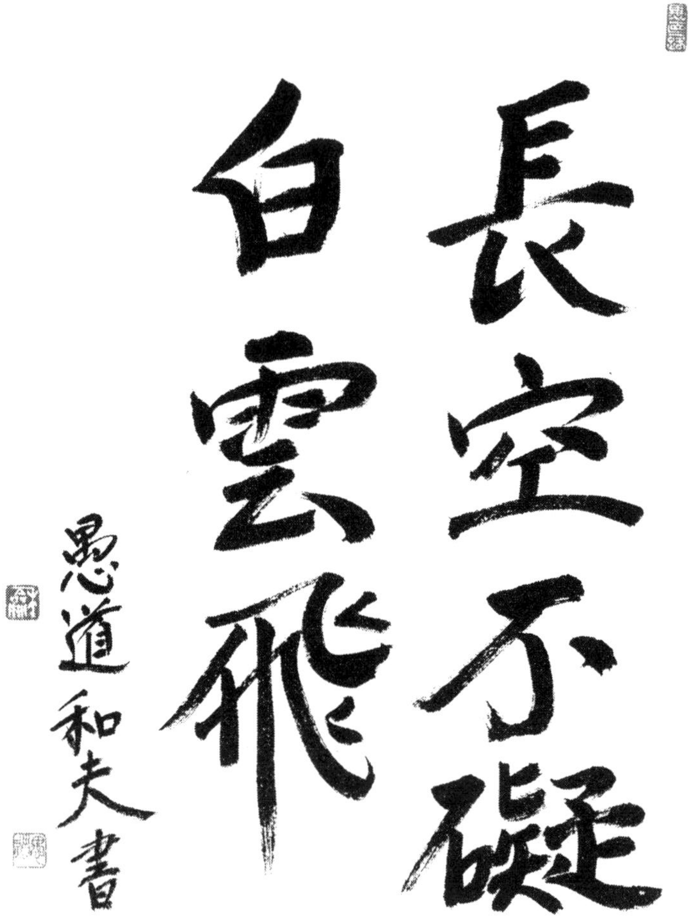

長空不礙
白雲飛

愚道 和夫書

*The sky doesn't hinder the clouds.*

## Chapter Five

## The Sky Doesn't Hinder the Clouds

*Friday, April 27, 2012*
Yesterday, I traveled by plane from Tokyo to Fukuoka, a city on the southernmost main island of Japan called Kyushu. A bus took me from Fukuoka Airport in the direction of Kumamoto. I got off at a bus stop in the countryside, where Father Franco Sottocornola, a Jesuit priest, picked me up with his car and brought me to the Catholic retreat and interreligious dialogue center Shinmeizan. It's a beautiful place on a hill in a forest surrounded by valleys and mountains. I will stay here for a one-week retreat in a traditional Japanese room with a straw mat floor and sliding paper doors.

This week, it's only Father Franco and me staying here. Today the hills are bathed in sunshine, and we have morning prayer outdoors. Then we celebrate the Eucharist in the main building, called *hondo* in Japanese.

After having received Christ in bread and wine, we eat breakfast and wash dishes together in silence. Then we have a period of working meditation, called *samu*. My chore is to pick up leaves from the stone steps and gravel path by hand, one at a time, and put them in a cardboard box. At the same time, other leaves are falling from the trees. Father Franco rakes the gravel in the rock garden. The birds are singing. I feel happy and grateful to be here.

~

Father Franco was born in 1935 in Bergamo, Italy. He was a professor of philosophy and liturgy in Parma for many years, and in 1978, he came to Japan as regional superior of the Xaverian Missionaries. He stayed for a year at a Buddhist temple near Kumamoto before he founded Shinmeizan, where he lives, works, prays, and celebrates the Eucharist to this day.

The word *Eucharist* comes from a Greek word meaning "thanksgiving." At the last supper with the disciples, before his suffering, Jesus Christ took bread, gave thanks, broke it, and gave it to the disciples, saying, "This is my body given for you; do this in remembrance of me" (Luke 22:19). Then he took a cup of wine, gave thanks, offered it to them, and said, "Drink from it, all of you. This is my blood of the covenant, which is poured out for many for the forgiveness of sins" (Matt. 26:27–28). Then they sang a hymn together before they went out to the Mount of Olives.

After many years of exploration of how the Eucharist and zazen relate to each other, Father Franco wrote an article, "Zazen and Adoration of the Eucharist," which was published in the spring 1995 issue of the *Japan Missionary Times*. He wrote:

> The sacramental silence of the broken bread kept in the Tabernacle of God's presence to us is an invitation to go beyond all words, all imagination and all images, beyond all that divides or separates, beyond all objects to the perfect communion of life and love, which the mystics have spoken to us about. Through the Son to the Father in the Spirit, that is: through the Word to Silence in Love.
>
> As we have seen above, silence is the deep nature of zazen. Silence of the voice, silence of the mind, silence of our whole being in the self-emptying death of the ego. It

is this deep, radical, total silence which can open our existence, our whole being, emptied of its own being (or selfishness), to the perfect communion with the silent Christ of the Tabernacle, sacrament of the Word of God who takes us to the Silence of the Father in a mystical union which is beyond words, images, and all created things.

During my early travels and training periods at Buddhist retreats, I noticed that I felt more and more drawn to my religious roots and life as a Christian. With help from Zen practice and teachings, I learned an approach to language and life that made the words and forms in the church come alive to me in new ways. I was no longer only focusing on the pointing finger, and I had become more open to explore what the finger was pointing at. Meditation helped me approach Christ not just as an idea about the past or the future but as reality here and now. I began to explore and reconnect with Christianity as a way of life and a practice. It took me several years, but step-by-step I connected with Christian friends and the forms of the church.

In the beginning of the process, my roots were weak. Sometimes I met representatives of the church with religious ideas that made me want to leave the church completely. But then somehow, a couple of weeks later, I was back there again.

With time and experience, and with many ups and downs, my roots grew stronger and deeper. I found my way back to the Church of Sweden, and I was touched to the heart by how warmly I was received despite my different background and sometimes different approach.

I think of Christianity, including the Bible, as a huge painting that has been painted by billions of hands over thousands of years. It's a painting that all Christians are baptized to be a part of and to continue painting together. During different times and situations in my life, I turn to different parts of the painting. For inspiration and consolation, my eyes rest on some parts more often than others.

The Christian painting does include ugly strokes of violence and prejudice toward others, based on, for example, gender, sexuality, religion, and ethnicity. From the beginning, the church was never a fixed, perfect entity. It's a living body, and we have an opportunity today to prevent more dark strokes from being added to the picture.

And, to me, the center of the Christian painting is shining like the sun. In my eyes, it shines with the message of God's love; a love that's not just a feeling, but I can't find a better word. It's a love that is given and that we are called to help manifest in the world. As a Christian, this is the center to where I turn. This center is the beginning: it is what I pray to remember on the way, and it is what I practice returning to, again and again.

I believe being baptized into this painting, and then relating to the life of Jesus Christ, as we do in the Eucharist, is the common ground of Christianity, despite all the different interpretations and denominations it holds. To me, it isn't about being right or wrong, but about relating to God through Christ together with others.

I consider my Christian faith to be more like music and art and less like law and mathematics. The truth of mathematics is great and very effective for building computers and many other things, but it doesn't fit all dimensions of life. Jesus is truth to me in the sense that his life touches mine in ways that mathematics can't reach. I believe the heart of that truth is that God is love, somehow the string that all pearls are strung on is love, beyond my understanding. Living with that faith in Christ is how I'm a Christian.

Neither Christianity nor the practice of meditation should be about creating some kind of club for perfect or "right" people. Christian life isn't about being better than anyone else or always having the right words to say. With all my misunderstandings and shortcomings and with all that is broken in me and around me—the cracks and the scars—I believe living a Christian life is about somehow giving ourselves to loving service in the footsteps of Christ.

Jesus enjoyed visiting other homes, and he said that in God's house there are many rooms (John 14:2). I'm grateful for my experiences of different religious traditions. I feel enriched from having shared meals with different families and met several streams of thought and practice in my life. It has made me who I am. The church is my religious home, with its strengths and weaknesses. But I also know that there are many other wonderful homes, religious or not.

Earlier in my life, I had more self-centered and exclusive ideas about religious truth. But as Nishijima Roshi once said to me, "The universe isn't that narrow." A cloud can enjoy feeling at home in a certain form, but it can never be closer to or farther away from the sky. I believe there is nothing that can separate anyone from God's love (Rom. 8:39), just like a cloud can never be separate from the sky. Heaven isn't closer to some of the clouds; it embraces us all.

In the summer of 2010, six years after receiving dharma transmission from Nishijima, I completed the required studies and training and was ordained as a priest in the Evangelical Lutheran Church of Sweden. It was a sunny day in June. My family and parents, my parents-in-law, and a few friends joined me at Luleå Cathedral in the north of Sweden, and the bishop of the Luleå diocese led the ordination ceremony for us new deacons and priests.

One of the priest vows is to live among people as a witness to God's love. Even though I continuously fail at embodying it, I feel comforted and challenged by remembering the direction of that fundamental vow. I like to think of it when I put on the priest collar in the morning.

⁓

> Dear friends, let us love one another, for love comes from God. Everyone who loves has been born of God and knows God. Whoever does not love does not know God, because God is love.
> —1 John 4:7–8

*A child of fire comes to get fire.*

## Chapter Six
## A Child of Fire Comes to Get Fire

*Saturday, April 28, 2012*
Father Franco and I are having morning prayer outside while the sun is rising over the valleys, fields, and forested hills. Afterward, I'm invited to join a memorial service for a visiting Japanese family's dead husband and father. After the service, we eat breakfast together with the family, and then I return to silence and samu. New leaves have fallen onto the stone steps and gravel path. I take the cardboard box and start picking them up, one by one.

―

There is a story in the Zen Buddhist tradition of a worried man who asks his meditation teacher about life and death. The teacher replies with a question: "Where are they?" (Shinji Shobogenzo, book two, case sixty-six). Similarly, Nishijima Roshi once wrote to a dying friend, "I'm sorry if my words sound a bit harsh, but please enjoy the fact that you are living right now."

When my ideas of life and death make me worry, I'm helped by being reminded that life is completely here and now. But it doesn't change the fact that sickness and dying are also completely here and now, sometimes along with indescribable suffering in this present moment.

Father Franco explained the meaning of the rock garden to me. The garden represents a pond. The raked gravel represents ripples on the surface of the water. These waves symbolize the relative, temporary, and changing nature of reality. The heavy rocks that rise from the gravel symbolize the absolute and eternal side. They are two sides of the same coin—rocks and waves, together in the garden.

Nishijima said, "Both true." A single coin has two sides, like two hands joined together in gassho or prayer. The form of single wave is impermanent, empty of a permanent and separate self, but it is born and part of the ocean, which is always full of everything.

In "Shunju" in the Shobogenzo, Dogen Zenji quoted Zen Master Engo Kokugon's words: "A bowl rolls around a pearl, and the pearl rolls around the bowl. The absolute in the relative, the relative in the absolute." And when I asked Nishijima how a fish knows she is swimming in water, he said, "Everything is in a situation like that."

On one of the rocks in the garden at Shinmeizan stands a statue of a woman holding a child in her arms. They are turned toward the raked gravel. It's Mary holding Jesus, her beloved newborn child. To me, their embrace is an image of both safety and vulnerability, heaven and earth.

I believe one of my deepest existential mistakes has been thinking that we have to achieve or earn to be a spark in the great fire, or a wave on the great ocean. In that sense, I have been much like a child of fire trying to get fire. I have often been a wave trying to find water and a cloud struggling to achieve the sky. But the apostle Paul wrote that whether we live or die, we belong to God (Rom. 14:7–8).

Mary and Jesus are here, in and with the whole garden, among both its ripples and rocks. In life and death, here with you and me. In the midst of the ocean, an eternal shore.

The statue is called Maria Kannon because the image of Mary is similar to images of a Buddhist *bodhisattva* called Kannon in Japanese. According to legend, she is a living being who has attained the possibility to become free from this world and its suffering and death but has chosen to stay and help free all others first. Many Zen temples have a statue of Kannon, venerated as the bodhisattva of compassion. Nishijima said that Kannon is a symbol of the character of the universe. Her name means "she who hears all the cries of the world," and sometimes she is portrayed with many eyes and arms, symbolizing that she sees all suffering and reaches out to save all.

A Buddhist nun once told me that when she bows to Kannon, she bows to the quality of compassion and loving-kindness in all beings. I believe it's possible to bow to images of Buddha or Christ and to each other in a similar way.

When the cold and darkness of winter fall over my hometown, everything is covered in a thick blanket of countless white snowflakes and ice. It's dark outside when I leave for work in the morning, and it's already dark again when I go home. The trees, fields, lakes, and rivers, everything looks completely sterile and dead in the snow, and it seems impossible that anything will survive to ever live and grow again.

Then spring arrives with her warm rays of light that melt the ice, and the flowers show themselves. They were never really gone, but waiting for the right circumstances to bloom again. And they will bloom again.

To me, this is the resurrection of Christ: cold, death, and darkness won't prevail, and love, light, and life will bloom again. When we're being still and we look patiently, even in the midst of frozen winter, it's possible to see the flowers in the snow. We can see that the flowers of last summer and the flowers of the coming spring are free from the concepts of separate being or nonbeing and free from the ideas of different and the same. When we see this reality, we can see that we can't be separate, and that, somehow, we will always have one another.

Last spring, I returned to Plum Village monastery in France again. A long-time friend of mine was dying at a nursing home in Umeå, and when I last saw her before going to France, she was worried. She was afraid of what was happening, but one of the last things she said to me was, "It's OK. I think it's OK." And then she said that it's probably more dangerous to be born than to die because when we are born, we can end up anywhere. After a few days of practicing meditation in the monastery, I wrote a letter to her:

> My dear friend,
> I'm writing to you from a monastery in France, where I'm staying for a one-week retreat. Here in France, spring is in full bloom. In the dining hall, there is a calligraphy painting that says, "A cloud never dies." The cloud changes form depending on the circumstances, but it never dies—just like the flowers go to sleep in the winter and then

show themselves again in the spring. In all the difficult changes you are going through now, please remember that the flowers will return again, and that through all seasons, you are in God's loving arms.

After returning home, I had the opportunity to sit with my friend, hold her hand, and talk to her. I'm not sure if she could hear me or not, but I talked about the memories we shared. I told her how the snow had disappeared and how beautiful spring was outside the window. Her heart stopped beating the next morning.

When I first began serving as a hospital priest, I was worried about how I would react with dead bodies, and especially with the dead body of a child. I was worried that I would collapse in tears, or that I wouldn't be able to enter the room. But with time I noticed that I can be present in situations like that. I believe meditation can help us move a bit more slowly and find space in our hearts to both break and reconnect.

My simple words fall short, but after about a year at the hospital church I wrote a poem:

> A stillborn child in my hands.
> My hands are small, yours even smaller,
> and only love.
> Your little nose,

our prayers, tears, and hymns.
Please don't be afraid,
you and I are more than this.
We are in greater hands than our own.
So we were even before our parents were born,
and the flowers will bloom again.

---

If I go up to the heavens, you are there;
if I make my bed in the depths, you are there.
If I rise on the wings of the dawn,
if I settle on the far side of the sea,
even there your hand will guide me,
your right hand will hold me fast.
If I say, "Surely the darkness will hide me
and the light become night around me,"
even the darkness will not be dark to you;
the night will shine like the day,
for darkness is as light to you.
—Psalm 139:8-12

*Not to know is the most direct and familiar.*

## Chapter Seven

## Not to Know Is the Most Direct and Familiar

*Sunday, April 29, 2012*
Shinmeizan isn't far from Nagasaki, where the second of two atomic bombs was dropped on August 9, 1945. It's also an area where many Christians were persecuted and killed for their faith in the sixteenth and seventeenth centuries. Today, I'm going for a silent walk in Nagasaki's Peace Park and Atomic Bomb Museum. Near the hypocenter of the explosion stands a tall statue called the Prayer Monument for Peace. The statue has one folded leg symbolizing prayer and meditation and one extended leg symbolizing the initiative to stand up to help one another. I stand silent for a while in front of the statue. The only words that come to mind are a form of the Sanskrit mantra *Om shanti*

*shanti shanti*. So I pray: "Peace. Peace. Peace. Amen."

～

When I was living with Nishijima Roshi in the dojo, I once went by Shinkansen bullet train to visit the Peace Park and Atomic Bomb Museum in Hiroshima, where the first atomic bomb fell on August 6, 1945. That night, after having seen images in the museum of the most unspeakable suffering, I was deeply upset. In the hotel room, on a small piece of paper, I wrote a sentence that has stayed with me ever since: "God is reality, truth and the whole." It's just a short statement with big words, but I needed to write it down. It came from my need for reconciliation with the fact that suffering and death are also in God, beyond my understanding.

From a prison cell, the apostle Paul wrote to a small congregation in Greece that God's peace transcends all understanding (Phil. 4:7). I don't understand, and I need simple, human images in order to cope and relate. I need to see Mary and Jesus standing in the rock garden, but equally important to me, I need them to grow from the soil of not knowing.

Later on, in the same evening, I shaved my head with a razor over the hotel room sink. My hair was already short, but for some reason, shaving it felt like a ritual to manifest what I had written on that small piece of paper. The next day, I went on a boat to a nearby island called Miyajima and walked up and down the hills among the rocks and trees. It helped me release more of the tensions from the day and night before, and I returned to Tokyo the following day. When Nishijima saw me back in the dojo, he laid his hand on his own shaved head, smiled, and said, "Beautiful."

At a place called Gethsemane, when Jesus was deeply troubled and sorrowful because he had understood something about what was going to happen to him on the cross, he went away from the disciples, fell with his face to the ground, and prayed to God: "My Father, if it is possible, may this cup be taken from me. Yet not as I will, but as you will" (Matt. 26:39).

Prayer, to me, is an open space where we're free to pour out our heart as it is, into God's hands. Some things we express with words, and we can pour out the rest in silence. And sometimes there is only silence. God is love, and when we pray to God, we train our heart and mind to turn in the direction of love.

Religion, however, isn't always turning in the direction of love. After the attacks in New York on September 11, 2001, I was troubled and concerned with how religion can become a destructive and violent force. I wanted to understand more about how and why it happens, and I applied to the master's degree program in peace studies at the University of Bradford in England with the intention of pursuing an academic career.

After graduating from Bradford in 2003, I received a scholarship for studying interreligious dialogue in Indonesia, where I got to know inspiring professors and friends, both Christian and Muslim. The following year, I returned to Indonesia and enrolled as a doctoral student at Gadjah Mada University's Department for Social and Political Studies in Yogyakarta. I lived and worked in Sweden and traveled to Indonesia for weeks or months of field studies every semester for about three years.

At the Institute for Interfaith Dialogue in Yogyakarta, I asked a young Muslim volunteer how it's possible to have dialogue for peace with violent individuals and groups. She replied, "It's impossible, but we have to do it." I was impressed with her courage and determination, and I hoped that my research could be helpful in some way. I decided to also try to get in touch with one of the allegedly violent groups.

My Indonesian Muslim friend and translator, Jamil Gunawan, helped me arrange a meeting with the leaders of an organization called Majelis Mujahidin. I was nervous and didn't really know what to expect the first time Jamil and I exited the taxi outside their headquarters in the outskirts of

Yogyakarta. On a wall behind a palm tree, I saw a big sign that said, "The Council of Mujahedeen for Islamic Law Enforcement."

On the front door, there were words in a language that I couldn't understand, but I recognized the word *jihad*. On the same door, as well as on stickers and T-shirts in the small shop behind it, I saw printed images of an open book with a sword in front of it. While waiting for our meeting, I looked through a couple of issues of the organization's magazine. I didn't understand the text, but I saw images of guns and war scenes.

After several interviews with the executive leaders, I was allowed to go to the Al-Mukmin Islamic boarding school in Ngruki to meet with Abu Bakar Bashir, the religious head of Majelis Mujahidin. Ngruki is a small town near a city called Solo, about an hour by car from Yogyakarta. During our meeting, Bashir mostly talked about Sharia law, a religious legal system that he said comes directly from God. The punishments he wanted to implement included flogging and cutting off hands. He referred to non-Muslims as *kafir*, which is an Arabic word meaning "infidel" or "unbeliever."

It seemed to me that Bashir thought he had access to answers to almost everything. In that sense, he also reminded me of some Christian priests I had met in the church. For every question, he had a fixed set of religious laws and truths. I met with

Bashir once every year for three years, and at the end of every one of our meetings, he told me that I should become Muslim.

After my third and last meeting with Bashir, Jamil and I stood in the school yard waiting for a taxi. I was feeling low and heavy after listening to Bashir. I felt empty, and my research felt worthless.

I like the Swedish word *underbart*. *Under* means "wonder," and *bart* means "naked" or "uncovered." It's similar to the English word *wonderful*, full of wonder, but the word *underbart* literally means "uncovered wonder."

In the Ngruki school yard, a group of children were playing with a small ball. They were laughing and kicking it to one another over a net, and they let me join in for a while. I was not very good at the game, but we laughed and had fun. Suddenly, I felt reconnected with life's uncovered wonder again.

When the disciples asked Jesus who was the greatest in the kingdom of heaven, he called a child to come and stand among them. Jesus said to the disciples that they had to change and become like little children in order to enter it (Matt. 18:2–3). But the Bible text doesn't say what the child was doing when Jesus called for her. I like to think that Jesus saw that she was playing. Perhaps kicking a small ball over a net.

From my meetings with the leaders of Majelis Mujahidin, playing with the children that day is a memory that I cherish. It was underbart.

While I was a doctoral student in Indonesia, I also got in touch with the Asian Muslim Action Network (AMAN) based in Thailand. I met with the organization's leader, Mr. Muhammad Abdus Sabur, at its headquarters in Bangkok. I learned that AMAN is working for peace, gender equality, and human rights based on the same religious tradition and scriptures as Majelis Mujahidin. Instead of images of war, *Amana Magazine*, the organization's publication, had articles on, for example, peace studies courses and women's equal right to sports.

Meeting both AMAN and Majelis Mujahidin as two different expressions of Islam reinforced my conviction that compassion here and now is always more important and holy than any other religious idea, no matter how old it is or by whom it is written. It seems to me that Jesus had this approach (Matt. 22:36–40; Mark 3:1–5; John 8:1–11; John 13:34), and I try my best to read the scriptures in this light.

I can't even imagine what my life would be like without written text and spoken language, but there are often too many words. Sometimes when we know too much, there is less open space for wonder. Father Franco said that a bird needs two wings to fly—both words and silence. Flying happens in the balance of the two and makes it possible to see a wider perspective. I used to think that it was through a perfect combination of words that I could find and hold on to God, but it came to be in the meditative space of silence and not knowing that my experience is most familiar and direct.

The universities I attended abroad were compelling to me, to some extent, I believe, because a part of me wanted to have social status and a successful career. But with time, I realized that I'm not a very good academic researcher. I enjoyed field studies and meetings, but I was struggling with reading and writing long academic texts. I felt drawn back to the church and family life in Sweden, and I let go of my academic ambitions.

---

> People were bringing little children to Jesus for him to place his hands on them, but the disciples rebuked them. When Jesus saw this, he was indignant. He said to them, "Let the little children come to me, and do not hinder them, for the kingdom of God belongs to such as these. Truly I tell you, anyone who will not receive the kingdom of God like a little child will never enter it." And he took the children in his arms, placed his hands on them and blessed them.
> —Mark 10:13–16

*The moaning of dragons among withered trees.*

## Chapter Eight

## The Moaning of Dragons among Withered Trees

*Monday, April 30, 2012*
It's a rainy day. After morning prayer and silent breakfast, I'm picking up leaves again, this time with a little help from the wind, which sweeps some of the leaves off the path. And the wind also makes more of them fall from the trees. This morning, Father Franco asked me to do samu for half an hour and then stop. He had noticed how old habits were pushing me to try to be effective and finish the job. But working meditation isn't about that. He said it's part of the morning prayer—and not about results.

～

There is an old story about a man in a wagon being pulled by five wild running horses, representing the five senses. They rush by a woman on the side of the road, and she calls out to him, "Where are you going?" The man in the wagon replies, "I have no idea—ask the horses!"

In my experience, first of all, meditation helps us to stop. It gives us a chance to return to the body, to posture and breathing. In that space, it's possible to listen to what thoughts and emotions are moving within. And by paying attention and being still with whatever is present in us, those thoughts and emotions lose a little of their power over us, and we become freer.

My friend Richard said to me that the samu I did at Shinmeizan would have been easier if the cardboard box had no bottom. We laughed, and Richard is probably right. Then there would have been no possibility for results. I believe the challenge and key to this practice is to see, accept, and receive every leaf, one at a time, and then to bring the same approach into everyday life. One moment, one meeting, and one leaf at a time, without too much attachment to results. "There is a time for everything, and a season for every activity under the heavens" (Eccles. 3:1).

The Epistle of James says: "My dear brothers and sisters, take note of this: Everyone should be quick to listen, slow to speak" (James 1:19). On one of my first days as a hospital priest, my colleague and mentor Anders Dahlqvist recommended that

I enter rooms, meetings, and situations at the hospital with empty hands. He said doing this means putting down my toolbox, theories, and ambitions for results, and entering the patient's room with an open presence, not knowing, being an open room myself. It means practicing being present with empty hands, able to listen and receive—just like with the leaves on the stone steps and gravel path at Shinmeizan.

Nishijima Roshi told me a story about a man who was very interested in dragons. The man in the story collected images, statues, and books about dragons. His house was full of them. Then one day, a real dragon came walking down the street and walked by his house. Through an open window she saw many beautiful images of dragons in the house, and she thought to herself, "This must be the home of someone who loves dragons very much. If I visit him, I'm sure he will be very happy." The curious dragon stuck her head through the open window to say hello, but when the man saw the dragon, he was so terrified that he fainted and fell down on the floor.

In "Zazenshin" in the Shobogenzo, Dogen Zenji wrote that "more than we love a carved dragon, we should love the real dragon." At first, I thought the only point of Nishijima's story was that I should not be preoccupied with constructed images of reality, of God, in order not to fall down on the floor.

Now I think that it's also about keeping the window open. I collect images of life, and I fall down on the floor sometimes. And just like the man in the house, I want to keep my window open. Meditation helps me with that.

At one time when I traveled home from Indonesia to Sweden, I changed flights in Hong Kong and took the opportunity to stay for a week at a Christian retreat and dialogue center called Tao Fong Shan. Just like Shinmeizan, it's located in a forest on the top of a mountain, and it's built like a temple. At Tao Fong Shan, the resident priest, Reverend John Lemond, told me that in one of the Chinese Bible translations, the Greek word *logos*, which can be translated as the "word of God," is translated as Tao (John 1:1).

The beginning of the ancient Taoist book, the Tao Te Ching, says that the Tao that can be spoken isn't the real Tao. In that sense, the Chinese Bible translation that Reverend Lemond referred to emphasizes that logos represents more than printed or spoken words. It's also mountains and rivers, leaves on a gravel path, and the moaning among withered trees.

~

> The heavens declare the glory of God; the skies proclaim the work of his hands.

Day after day they pour forth speech; night after night they reveal knowledge.
They have no speech, they use no words; no sound is heard from them.
Yet their voice goes out into all the earth, their words to the ends of the world.
—Psalm 19:1–4

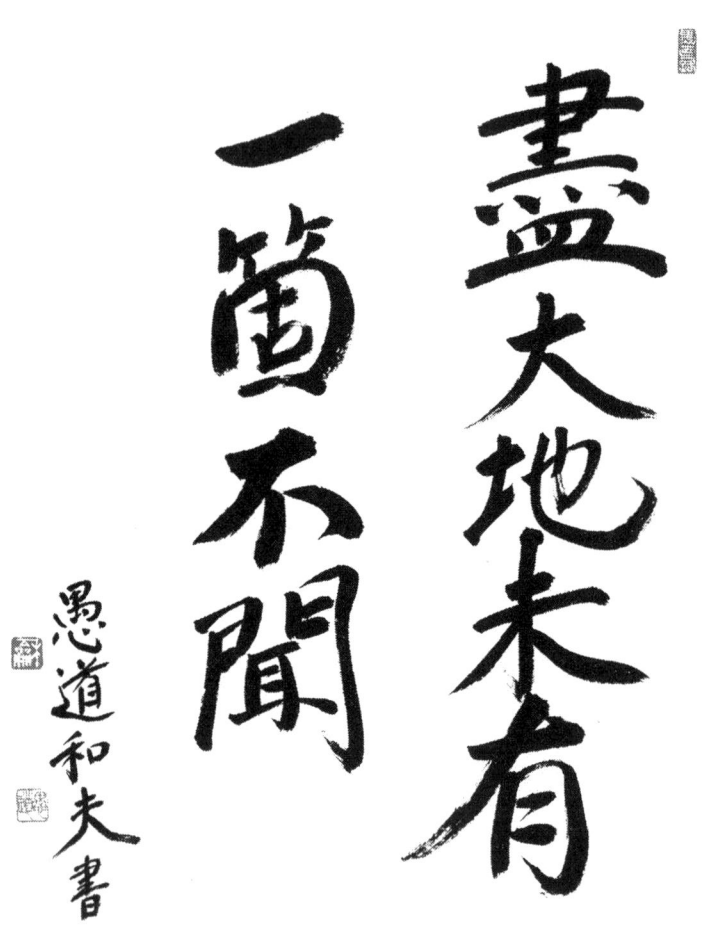

*There is no one who doesn't hear them.*

## Chapter Nine
## There Is No One Who Doesn't Hear Them

*Tuesday, May 1, 2012*
Today Father Franco and I are visiting the Seimeizan Schweitzer Buddhist Temple in the nearby city of Tamana, where he lived many years ago. It's also called the Temple of Reverence for Life because its late founder, Tairyu Furukawa Roshi, dedicated his life to protesting social injustice; he visited prison inmates and campaigned against the death penalty in Japan and around the world.

―

The first time I visited a prison was in 2004, on a carefully guided tour of the modern Fuchu Prison in Japan, as part of a UN University course on human rights. We listened to a presentation by the staff, and then we walked in a tight group with guards through an area where the male inmates worked in silence. We were told that the women in our group had to walk in the center, surrounded by us men. No contact. Just walking by and looking at the facilities and the inmates while they were working.

The second time, in 2005, was different. My wife, Emmy, was writing an article on Bogor Prison, near Jakarta, Indonesia, for Amnesty Press, and I joined her as a photographer. We came to the rundown prison together with a Christian chaplain and his assistants. For a few hours we were allowed to move around certain areas and talk with some of the female inmates. One of the prison guards followed us around and served as our translator. Some of the women seemed to be very young, and the prison was overcrowded.

In the minivan on our way back to Jakarta, I asked the chaplain what words in the Bible he finds most comfort in. Without hesitation, he quoted from the end of the Bible, where God says, "I am making everything new" (Rev. 21:5).

Emmy and I had been living in Stockholm for a few years, but in the beginning of 2006, we moved up north again, back to Umeå. For a couple of years, I had been working night shifts at Arlanda Airport's post office, with bags and boxes that had to get on the right planes to their destinations.

Back in Umeå, I applied for every job that I could find. In the spring of 2006, after a couple of months of loading crates at a car-manufacturing company, I got a job as a remand prison officer in Umeå.

According to the Swedish Prison and Probation Service, a remand prison is a custody facility for persons who are waiting for a trial or a place in a prison. The court decides what contact a person on remand may have with the world outside the prison, and restrictions might include visits or telephone calls being monitored or fully denied. The prisoner may also be denied access to television, radio and newspapers.

From 2006 to 2010, I worked at the remand prison in Umeå, mostly night shifts, while undergoing priest studies and training. Behind the prison walls, I met suffering, loneliness, and death in a closer and more intense way than ever before in my life. What troubled me the most was the injuries the prisoners sometimes inflicted on themselves, their anguish, and a suicide that cut to my heart.

At the prison, I was fortunate to have compassionate and insightful colleagues by my side. One of the first things they taught me was to always remember, before opening a door, that it could be me in the prison cell.

But some doors were more difficult to open

than others, and in the beginning, I especially disliked one of them. Knowing what the inmate had allegedly done repulsed me, and the smell from his room made me feel sick every time I had to open the door. And then one day, I had to take him to a communal room for an hour and have a cup of coffee with him. I didn't want to do it, but it was my job and I had to.

At first our conversation was quite numb. But after sitting down together for a while, something happened. He began to tell me about his life and his childhood. I listened, and it sunk into my heart that he had once been a little child, just like me. If I had grown up like him and been through the same experiences that he had, I have no idea who I would have become. Probably not very different from him.

Dogen Zenji wrote that the body is like a dewdrop on a blade of grass ("Fukan-zazengi" in the Shobogenzo). It struck me how fragile I am, how fragile is the construction of myself, and how fragile is the web of life that we share together. And in this shared fragility we could meet, the inmate and I, and my feeling of aversion toward him as a person was transformed.

Sitting down and paying attention helped me see that not only could it be me in the prison cell but also, in a sense, that it *is* me. It helped me to receive in a new way Jesus's teaching about loving my enemy (Matt. 5:43–44) and to see that my so-called enemy isn't separate from me.

In Kyoto, more than a decade ago, I met with Zen teacher and American studies professor Tom Wright. I had brought with me many questions and a small recorder, and we sat down at a café. During the Vietnam War, Professor Wright had been a conscientious objector in the United States and a protestor against the war. He told me about one time after the war when he met an old friend who had served as a soldier in Vietnam:

> All I could do was to embrace him, and he embraced me, too. He was crying and I was crying, just because we were so happy that both of us were still alive. Gustav, how can we become big enough people so that we could also not condone things that Hitler did but still embrace every human being regardless of what they have done? How can we nurture our life to be that big, to include all? That is my practice.

One time at the remand prison in Umeå, there was an inmate who had an especially violent history. My colleagues and I were a bit tenser when we opened the door to his room. One evening, when another officer and I were going from room to room, serving fruit and tea, we stopped a little longer with him. Instead of just giving him an apple and closing the door, we stopped and asked him how he was doing. To our surprise, he showed us photographs and told us about his life. We listened for about fifteen minutes before we had to continue on to the next room.

Once a week, every inmate at the remand prison got ninety Swedish kronor, the equivalent of about eleven US dollars. It's not much, and it's often used for buying two packs of cigarettes. The following evening, at the beginning of the next night shift, my colleague and I were serving fruit and tea again. Once again, we opened the door to the same man's cell. This time he said he had something for us. He had used part of his weekly money to buy us a bar of chocolate because we had listened to him the night before.

My first impulse was not to accept his gift, because I thought he needed the chocolate more than we did. Fortunately, we quickly realized that his need for connecting and giving us something was greater than his need for chocolate. My colleague and I received his gift, thanked him, and enjoyed sharing the chocolate later that night. In a way, his gift has stayed with me ever since, as a reminder of what those few minutes of stopping and listening meant to the three of us.

In "Bodaisatta-shishobo" in the Shobogenzo, Dogen wrote that "kind speech has the power to turn around the heavens; it is not merely the praise of ability." And Nishijima Roshi described the present moment as the sharp edge of a razor. On the razor's edge is a small pearl, and it can fall either to the left or right side. The sharp edge is our stage, the place where we can act and tip the balance of the pearl to either side.

When Nishijima and I talked about the miracle stories of healing in the gospels—the written accounts of the life of Jesus of Nazareth—he said that he was not very interested in whether such miracles had actually happened or not. But he said that every situation, even a very difficult one, can be changed a little bit for the better or for the worse, based on our actions in the present moment. And in that sense, there can be miracles here and now. Sometimes during difficult nights at the remand prison in Umeå, I thought of what Nishijima had said.

I don't think Jesus healed with some kind of magic, but I believe the point is that he healed with his presence and compassion. In meditation, we are being still, and we pay attention to the landscape within. But we can't force peace, forgiveness, or love to bloom—not in ourselves or anywhere else. All we can do is to practice keeping the window open, giving space and light and tending to the soil in a way that, when the conditions allow, the seeds of healing may be able to grow and bloom by themselves. Little by little, step by step. Right foot. Left foot. Falling down and beginning anew. You and me, one small miracle at a time.

The priestly blessing in the Hebrew Bible, which is often given at the end of Christian prayers and services, speaks of God's face being turned to us:

> The Lord bless you and keep you;
> the Lord make his face shine on you and be gracious to you;
> the Lord turn his face toward you and give you peace.
> —Numbers 6:24–26

Meditation is a way for me to practice turning my face to God's face, which I believe is always turned to us all. To me, it's an image that says we are all, ultimately, seen and held dear. In that sense, there is no one who doesn't hear it. There is no one who is not embraced by it, regardless of whether we are a prison inmate or a guard. But we can turn toward it or away from it, and the difference can be as wide as heaven or hell. When we turn away from it, we might not be able to see beyond our relative and temporary roles and situations. And when we turn to it, we can see that we are not only inmates and guards, but we are also boundless children of God, together. Turning our face to this reality makes it possible to sit and walk with more freedom, even behind prison walls.

~

> [Jesus said,] "What shall we say the kingdom of God is like, or what parable shall we use to describe it? It is like a mustard seed, which is the smallest of all seeds on earth. Yet when planted, it grows and becomes the largest of all garden plants, with such big branches that the birds can perch in its shade."
> —Mark 4:30–32

*All those who hear it free themselves of something.*

# Chapter Ten
## All those Who Hear It Free Themselves of Something

*Saturday, May 5, 2012*
After a week at Shinmeizan, I'm back in Tokyo again. Noodle restaurants, neon signs that I don't understand, and lots of electric wires line the streets. It's a national holiday in Japan, and I'm on my way to visit Toshoji Zen Temple. Thousands of people pass by me. The crowd is endless. And in every person, a heart and a story. In every person, smiles and tears, fear and love. In that sense, every person is just like me.

At Toshoji, in the middle of every period of zazen, one of the monks walks slowly around the room and hits everyone's back with a kyosaku stick. They hit harder here, compared to Rinsenji, and it's not optional. When the meditation gathering, called *zazenkai*, has come to an end, I stay and talk with one of the monks. He tells me that he practices zazen to prepare for weeks of intense sesshin at the temple, because during sesshin he can reach total enlightenment, called *kensho* or *satori* in Japanese.

---

Toshoji was one of the places I visited when I first came to Japan. At that time, the teacher, Tetsujyo Deguchi Roshi, told me a story about a young man who liked to look at his beautiful face in the mirror every day. But one day the mirror broke. He was very upset because he couldn't see his face anymore, and he thought that he had lost it. He ran around, desperately searching for his beautiful face. Others told him to stop running, that it was still there, but he couldn't see it and continued chasing after it in desperation. Then one of his friends grabbed him and tied him to a pole. He tied the ropes tightly and told him, again, that his beautiful face was there, but he still could not understand it. Then his friend slapped him in the face. In that moment, the young man felt his face and realized that it was still there, that it had been there all along. Tetsujyo Deguchi said that zazen is like being tied to a pole and slapped in the face.

In one sense, I think this story is a helpful image. We all share an inherent beauty of life, whether we see it or not. Inseparable. But in my experience, being tied to a pole and slapped in the face usually isn't a safe and sound way to peace. To a certain extent, discipline and effort are good companions on the way, but I believe they need to be balanced and walk hand in hand with surrender and playfulness. I think meditation practice shouldn't be just something that we push ourselves through, but more of a habit to enjoy.

After my first visit to Toshoji, back in early 2001, I went to stay for a short while in a Rinzai Zen temple near Kyoto. After a half-hour train ride from Kyoto station, past rivers and green hills, I arrived in a small town called Kameoka. From there, a local bus took me to the countryside, and after a short walk, I arrived at Kokusai Zendo at Tokoji Temple. The next morning, the abbot Gensho Hozumi Roshi and I sat down for a talk, and I asked him about enlightenment.

Gensho Hozumi said that satori isn't something that is somewhere to be found. It's also not just yours or mine; in a sense it's everybody's enlightenment. It's a commonality for all life and not about religious doctrines. He said that satori can be described as an experience of the fundamental unity of things. It's as if someone were sitting on a small island in the middle of a great ocean and the island gradually ceased to exist. We're no longer a separate part. We get a sense of unity, and then compassion is a natural state of mind.

Later on, in the dojo, I asked Nishijima about the goal of zazen. He said, "Yes, zazen has a goal, and the goal of zazen is zazen itself." When I continued to ask him about enlightenment, he said that there are two kinds. The first kind is the practice, zazen, in itself. The other kind, he said, comes gradually with maturity in the practice, but it's nothing to think or worry about at all.

Nishijima said that rigorous styles of Zen training are often closely related with idealistic goals, and I could relate. When I first began with Zen meditation, ideas similar to the image of tying and slapping were dominant in my practice. But in my experience, it created unwholesome tensions in me. And the tensions I carried within me easily spilled over to others that I met.

Now zazen, to me, isn't much about idealistic goals. If I could say only one thing, I would say that it helps me feel closer. In my experience, it helps me live more in touch with others, with myself, and with the place I'm in. It lets me return to more balance and to a greater sense of connection and unity with life as it is. And it helps me be a little more at ease in the continuous flow of receiving and letting go.

When our children were a few months old, I remember them sitting in the bathtub with water running from the tap. They were interested in the running water, and they tried to catch it with their small hands. I think all three of them used to do that. It was fun, but they were also a bit frustrated. They really wanted to catch and hold on to the running water. And I have tried to do the same with many things in life. I have tried to catch and hold on to something that is flowing.

The practice of meditation helps me live more anchored in the experience that this great, flowing now includes both the past and the future, my grandparents and future generations. I see their hands in mine. And at the same time, there is no present moment that we can catch and hold on to. That doesn't make it less real. It's actually what makes it real, and it's what makes every heartbeat possible.

Nishijima said that the present moment is a very short time, but it's also eternal. What we have is this moment together. It's empty of permanence, but its lack of permanence enables it to be full of everything. In this flowing oneness of emptiness and form, in God, all things hold together (Col. 1:17), and we live and move and have our being (Acts 17:28).

At one time, Shakyamuni Buddha sat before a large audience full of expectations, but for a long time he didn't say a word. Then he picked up a flower and held it quietly before the assembly. Nobody understood anything, and everyone looked bewildered, except one of his disciples, Mahakashyapa. His face shone with a gentle smile. According to legend, this moment is the origin of the Zen tradition.

All those who hear it free themselves of something. But as soon as we try to pin it down with sharp definitions, it has already slipped from our hands. When we sit down for meditation, it's not with words and ideas at the center. We sit down with the flower. It's a gateless gate; it's training in returning to that smile. And we're freed from something.

> All streams flow into the sea,
> yet the sea is never full.
> To the place the streams come from,
> there they return again.
> —Ecclesiastes 1:7

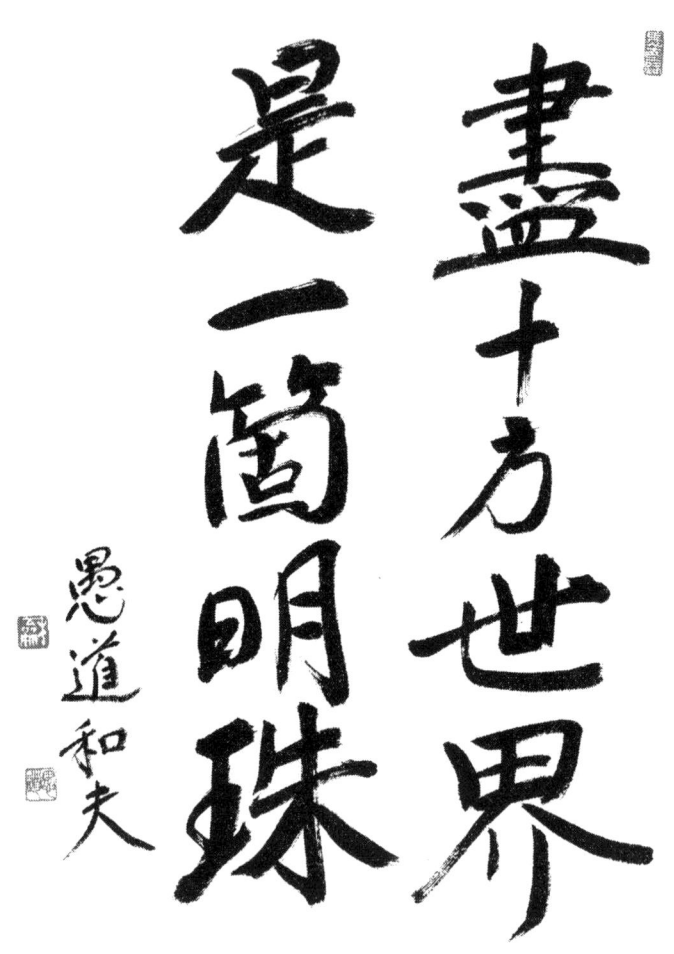

*The whole universe in all directions is just one brilliant pearl.*

## Chapter Eleven
## The Whole Universe Is One Brilliant Pearl

*Sunday, May 6, 2012*
I'm invited to join the Sunday service at the Japan Evangelical Lutheran Church in Shinjuku in Tokyo. Children are playing outside the church, and the sun is shining from a blue sky. The service is in Japanese, but the ritual form, the liturgy, and the melodies of some of the hymns are familiar to me. Sometimes, I can guess what they are saying, and I join quietly in Swedish.

Over the altar in the Shinjuku church hangs a combination of seven metal crosses, representing the last seven words of Jesus Christ. The crosses are dark and rough, but somehow, they make a bright reflection of light on one of the walls. The cross is a tool for execution, brutal beyond words,

> but it has become a reflection of light,
> a beacon of love.

---

I sometimes think of the horizontal line of the cross as the linear idea of time, moving from past to present and into the future, and the vertical line as space, connecting heaven and earth. The center of the cross, where the two lines meet, is this present time and space where Christ continues to live, die, and rise again with us all.

There is an old story called "Indra's Net." It's an infinite net, stretching out in all directions. In every little intersection, in every knot of the net, there is a pearl, and in every one of the infinite number of pearls are reflections of all the other pearls. Actually, not only reflections of them, but somehow they are also there, in each and every one. It sounds like a magical net in a fantasy story, but I think the pearls are much like you and me and this whole universe.

Dogen Zenji wrote that the whole moon and the whole sky are reflected in a dewdrop on a blade of grass, but the moon does not get wet, and the sky does not break the water ("Genjo-koan" in the Shobogenzo). The ten thousand complicated things are here, right in front of us, but they have never covered anything. The beautiful simplicity is also right here in front of us, now, and nothing has ever covered it. According to the Book of Psalms, King David wrote that God is all around us, and we're completely in God's hand (Ps. 139:5). When we somehow dig and search for God, I think, in a sense, we have lost the way, because God has never been hidden.

In Glasgow about ten years ago, at a conference on the psychology of religion, I met an old professor who had grown up in Czechoslovakia. He said that sometimes when his family had sat down together for dinner, they had no food to put on their plates. They were hungry and had nothing to eat, but they sat down at the dinner table and joined their hands in prayer anyway, and they gave thanks for being together and alive.

At the dojo in Japan, we all said *itadakimasu* together before a meal, which literally means, "I humbly receive." And at Shinmeizan, we always said a prayer before sitting down to eat. I like the habit of joining my palms together before a meal and bowing gently with a short prayer. Sometimes I just say quietly, "Thank you, God, for the food." And sometimes my prayer is a little longer—for everyone to have wholesome food on their plates, and to be able to enjoy being together and alive.

Jesus quoted Deuteronomy 8:3 and said that we don't live by bread alone, but we live from every word that comes from the mouth of God (Matt. 4:4).

One of my favorite dinners in Japan was the rice, tofu, soy sauce, and pickled cucumbers that I often bought at one of the many small convenience stores in Tokyo and Kyoto, and none of those pearls on my plate could have been there without one another. They couldn't have been there without the work of many people, and not without the countless little raindrops, the sunshine, and the mud. And neither can you and I.

In "Bodaisatta-shishobo" in the Shobogenzo, Dogen wrote:

> People have taken pity on stricken turtles and taken care of sick sparrows. When they saw the stricken turtle and the sick sparrow, they did not seek any reward from the turtle and the sparrow; they were motivated solely by helpful conduct itself. ...//... Helpful conduct is the whole Dharma. It universally benefits self and others.

On the Via Dolorosa, Latin for "the way of suffering," Jesus was forced to carry the cross on the way to his execution on Golgotha. In the Christian tradition, this is an image of God carrying the suffering of the world. At one point, Jesus fell down and could not get up. Then a man in the crowd, Simon of Cyrene, had to help Jesus carry the cross (Luke 23:26).

Sometimes, like Simon, we are able to help Jesus carry the cross. And sometimes we fall down and can't get up, and we need one another. In that sense, we can help God carry the suffering of the world. We can be the eyes, ears, and arms of Christ and Maria Kannon to one another. The whole universe is one pearl, and what makes it brilliant is love.

---

> The light shines in the darkness, and the darkness has not overcome it.
> —John 1:5

*Anzenkai*

## Chapter Twelve
## Anzenkai

*Friday, May 11, 2012*
After one long and two shorter flights, I'm back with my family in Umeå. It's early morning and I'm sitting still and walking slowly with Anzenkai again. After a round of sharing, we wash our teacups and put the cushions back in place. I step outside, and some people on bicycles ride by. The grass next to the buildings and sidewalks is both brown and green. It's time for me to go to work at the church, where the prayer candles already light up the morning.

～

In 2007, while visiting Nishijima Roshi in his apartment, I had an idea. I wanted to start an open and religiously independent network called Anzenkai that would support a daily meditation practice and provide a community for practitioners from a variety of traditions. Nishijima gladly supported the idea, and he made a calligraphy painting of the Japanese *an-zen-kai* characters for the group.

*An* means "peace," *zen* is meditation, and *kai* indicates a kind of organization or gathering of people. But it's also a play on words. *Anzen*, pronounced in the same way but written with different Japanese characters, is a common abstract noun meaning "safety." When he looked back at his experiences of war, Nishijima described zazen as a vehicle for peace. Meditation is a kind of peace work.

I began by arranging weekly meditation groups in Umeå, and I led our first sesshin in 2009, outdoors, on nearby Holmön Island. The meditation group grew, and more retreats followed. After a few years, it became clear to me that Anzenkai needed a basic definition of its foundation and direction. I began reflecting on what was fundamental to the group and its practice, and I ended up with four foundation stones and three guiding stars.

First of all, Anzenkai is an open and religiously independent network, not based on any particular religious creed. This is the first foundation stone: everyone is welcome. Some of us are Christians, some are Buddhists, and some belong to other religious traditions or none at all. It's a space for community across the boundaries of traditions, and we train together as friends, enriched by our diversity.

The main purpose and second foundation stone of Anzenkai is to support the daily practice of zazen and kinhin. To be a friendly and supportive community for the practice of sitting and walking meditation in everyday life.

In order to nourish the habit of daily meditation training, we arrange zazenkai. At the time of writing, we have weekly zazenkai in Umeå. We do two or three periods of zazen, with kinhin in between. Sometimes we also arrange sesshin or go to other retreats together. To arrange opportunities for practicing meditation together is the third foundation stone of Anzenkai.

The fourth foundation stone is the round of sharing that we have at the end of every zazenkai and once in every retreat day. Sitting and walking meditation can open up space in us for truly listening and being present with one another. I think the round of sharing is just as important as zazen and kinhin, and in my experience, they nourish each other.

At the end of zazenkai, we sit in a circle on the floor. We sit facing one another and sometimes with a cup of tea. Then the practice leader takes a piece of rock or something similar, holds it, and shares some thoughts or an experience related to the practice.

We share our own thoughts and experiences into the middle of the circle and not directed at any other person. With a few breaths of silence in between, we pass the stone on to the person sitting to our left. The person who is holding the stone can choose to speak or just hold it silently for a little while. Each and every one is free to use the kind of language that one is most comfortable with, religious or not.

The round isn't longer than a period of zazen, and we share the time with one another so that everyone is given space to speak. It isn't meant to be some kind of evaluation of the practice; it's an opportunity to share and listen from the heart. What is being said in the group stays in the group, and we don't tell others about what has been said during a round of sharing.

At the end of the round, when the stone is back where it started, there is usually time for some questions or casual conversation. Then we join our palms together and express our thanks to the group with a bow. We rise carefully from our seats and clean up together, and then we bring our practice out from the zendo and into everyday life.

Meditation isn't about competition or achievement. We practice letting go of ambition when we sit down for zazen. And at the same time, guiding stars can help us with intention, navigation, and direction in our practice.

Anzenkai's first guiding star is awareness. We practice returning with our awareness to the posture of the body and to just this breath, to this time and place, in order to look and listen, to pay attention, and to touch the intimately interconnected nature of life together here and now.

The second guiding star is friendship. We practice in order to be a good friend to others and to ourselves. Meditation isn't just for one's own benefit; it's also for the well-being of others, for us all. This star invites us to intertwine meditation with work, social service, family life, and other kinds of engagement in the world—not to inflate our ego but as an expression of what is touched in the practice.

The third guiding star is balance, which is a word that Nishijima frequently used. Human practice means human mistakes—inevitable falling and getting back up again. We practice where we are, just as the human beings we are, in a direction that lets life and meditation flow as one. Meditation training is about returning to balance in everyday life as it is, among both the flowers and the mud. It's not about pushing and chasing after too idealistic goals.

I think meditation is a kind of training in coming home to this moment and to this place. And sometimes it can also make it possible for us to help others feel more at home.

This book began with a poem from the Buddhist tradition on arriving, and I would like to end with a few words that I wrote when I first set out on this path.

> Snow-white moon in a circle cloud,
> full of things to say.
> Smiling in the dark above naked trees.
> Gratefully, I bow as I listen.
> Walking home.

It's something I wrote in a notebook one winter evening in Umeå, long before I had set foot in Japan. It's from when I started out—just as, in a sense, I would like to continue starting out, with a beginner's mind, again and again, throughout my life. In many ways, I'm still a mess, still stumbling along in life. And at the same time, I'm home.

---

> See! The winter is past;
> the rains are over and gone.
> Flowers appear on the earth;
> the season of singing has come,
> the cooing of doves
> is heard in our land.
> The fig tree forms its early fruit;
> the blossoming vines spread their fragrance.
> —Song of Songs 2:11–13

# Acknowledgments

I'm grateful for scholarships from the Church of Sweden and from the Scholarship Foundation for Studies of Japanese Society, which have supported this book project. Many thanks to Anna Steele, Anne Ormrot, Daniel Pettersson, Gustav Jacobsson, Johannes Nord, Jundo Cohen, Lars Segerstedt, Maria Klasson Sundin, Peter Rocca, Rune Ødegaard, Ruth Wieting, Ulf Dahne, Ylva Hansen, and Åsa Norin, who gave generously of their time and energy to read the manuscript for this book and helped me with valuable comments and insights during the writing process, and to Carl-Erik Engqvist, who helped me scan the calligraphic works.

This book is a weaving, written with gratitude to all its threads: my parents and brothers; teachers, colleagues, and friends; the Church of Sweden, Dogen Sangha, Plum Village, and Shinmeizan; everyone in Anzenkai; my family; and especially my wife, Emmy, who has put up with my travels and retreats throughout the years. With all my heart, thank you.

# Calligraphy References

Chapter one and two   Zen Master Reiun Shigon, quoted in "Keiseisanshiki" in the Shobogenzo, and quoted in book two, case fifty-five, in the Shinji Shobogenzo.

Chapter three   Zen Master Engo Kokugon, quoted in "Shinjingakudo" in the Shobogenzo.

Chapter four   An expression based on the teachings of Zen Master Tendo Nyojo, quoted, for example, in "Gyoji" in the Shobogenzo.

Chapter five   Zen Master Sekito Kisen, quoted in "Butsu-kojono- ji" in the Shobogenzo, and quoted in book two, case ninety-one, in the Shinji Shobogenzo.

Chapter six   Zen Master Seiho, quoted in "Bendowa" in the Shobogenzo, and quoted in book two, case twenty-two, in the Shinji Shobogenzo.

| | |
|---|---|
| Chapter seven | Zen Master Rakan Keichin, quoted in book two, case seventy-one, in the Shinji Shobogenzo. |
| Chapter eight | Zen Master Kyogen Chikan, quoted in "Ryugin" in the Shobogenzo, and quoted in book one, case twenty-eight, in the Shinji Shobogenzo. |
| Chapter nine | Zen Master Sozan Honjaku, quoted in "Ryugin" in the Shobogenzo, and quoted in book one, case twenty-eight, in the Shinji Shobogenzo. |
| Chapter ten | Zen Master Sozan Honjaku, quoted in "Ryugin" in the Shobogenzo, and quoted in book one, case twenty-eight, in the Shinji Shobogenzo. |
| Chapter eleven | Zen Master Gensa Shibi, quoted in "Ikka-nomyoju" in the Shobogenzo, and quoted in book one, case fifteen, in the Shinji Shobogenzo. |

Printed in Great Britain
by Amazon